OBJECTIVES + KEY RESULTS (OKR) LEADERSHIP

HOW TO APPLY SILICON VALLEY'S SECRET SAUCE TO YOUR CAREER, TEAM, OR ORGANIZATION

DOUG GRAY, PHD, PCC

Action Learning Associates, LLC
www.Action-Learning.com
Gray Publications
Franklin, TN, USA

TESTIMONIALS

"Doug's leadership training of the OKR process has been received positively by my sales team due to the coaching being simple, engaging and very effective."
Terry Fortner, VP Sales and Marketing, North America LKQ Corporation.

"Doug Gray makes the complex understandable. More important, he makes it doable."
Craig E. Aronoff, Ph.D., author, Chairman and co-founder, The Family Business Consulting Group, Inc.

"John Doerr's book *"Measure What Matters"* describes how OKRs (Objectives and Key Results) transformed Silicon Valley. With this new book, Doug builds on the OKR approach with practical and valuable guidance for individuals, teams and organizations. If you plan on implementing OKRs for your organization, you need this book."
John Mattox, PhD, author, Head of Talent Research, Metrics that Matter, Explorance

"The top five companies in Silicon Valley have an economic value as great as the United Kingdom. They must know something. Doug has uncovered their secrets in his *OKR Leadership* approach."
Jac Fitzenz, PhD, author, Founder Saratoga Institute and Human Capital Source

"Doug Gray provides readers with a 'moment of truth' concerning how we can transform lofty objectives into down-to-earth results."
James Dillon, co-Founder, Emerging Step

"Introducing the OKR framework has not only allowed us to align our company goals throughout the organization, but it has also provided an easy mechanism to give visibility into how we drive operational accountability. That visibility now exists for both our employees and supervisors. OKR Leadership has encouraged broader and more in-depth conversations about the right key results to drive individual or team objectives."

Justin Jude, Acting President, LKQ Corp, North America

"Doug's new book challenges me to be a leader and to practice leadership. This book provides a practical framework that will make you a more successful leader."

David Cardwell, SVP, IT Operations, F100 company

"Finally, a much needed leadership focus on the importance of clear objectives and specific, measurable results. This book will be useful not just for the present but throughout a practitioner's career."

Dave Vance, PhD, author, Executive Director, Center for Talent Reporting

"In his new and exciting book, *OKR Leadership*, Doug Gray shares how his proven techniques can help you move the needle to achieve the business outcomes you've been striving for. If you're ready for a transformation, then *OKR Leadership* is a must read!"

Sheri Bankston, VP, Alliance Safety Council

"History is littered with the graves of organizations who had the right strategy but were unable to execute. Lack of execution is a very real threat to every organization's survival. This is a very practical look at the

OKR system to accomplishing results. Written incredibly clearly, Doug Gray has brought OKR Leadership to life in a way that would benefit any organization."

Brian Underhill, Ph.D., author, Founder and CEO, CoachSource

The publisher, Gray Publications, 3482 Stagecoach Drive, Franklin, TN, USA is a product of Action Learning Associates, LLC.

www.Action-Learning.com

ISBN-13: 978-0-9758841-4-0 (e-Book) for $6.97 USD
ISBN-13: 978-0-9758841-6-4 (paperback) for $19.97 USD

Copy editing by NY Book Editors
Cover and interior formatting by eBookLaunch
Graphic designs by John Murdock

CONTENTS

Examples. Definitions. Challenges. Assumptions. Dialog. History. Facts.

Dialog. Objectives. Key results. KR formulas. OKR worksheet. Examples.

Dialog. Competitive market advantage. ISO human capital standards. Leadership Trust Index (LTI). Follower Trust Index (FTI). Psychological Capital (PsyCap). Hierarchies. Aspirations. Confusion. Feedback.

Dialog. Write and share your OKRs. Support the Vision and Strategy. Review at least quarterly. Use the AD-FITTM coaching process daily.

Dialog. Career lifespan. Career transition scoresheet. Organizational fit. Examples in your 20s, 30s, 40s and 50s.

Dialog. Leadership skills. Family-owned business leaders. Role confusion. Succession planning. Cost reduction. Organizational change.

Impact studies. Technology. Diversity. Positive Psychology. The OKR Leadership project 2020+.

LIST OF FIGURES BY CHAPTER

PREFACE

How do you keep track of what's important when you watch sports? Well, you use a scoreboard. Or a timer. Or a finish line. You **use *numbers* to measure what matters**. Then you boast about your favorite scores. In short, you know who wins because you know who had the better numbers. This book is written for readers and leaders with the same kind of focus — **you need to know what to measure so that you can win**.

Similarly, when you drive a car, you stay between the lines to reach your goal. When you drive on an interstate, you somehow avoid risks while hurtling through space at 70 mph with only plastic and 6 inches separating you from danger. You trust that countless strangers doing the same will not hurt you or your loved ones. You trust your strange Uber driver. Even those who drive in Paris, France around the Arc de Triumph somehow avoid risk without lines to guide their driving. When you drive around your local roundabout, you somehow create safety amid chaos. How do you avoid those risks? You collaborate. You assess risk. You make smart choices. This book is also written for readers **who need to avoid chaos and achieve outcomes**.

When you manage others, you try to maximize their productivity (e.g., effectiveness, efficiency or outcomes). Some days – and some relationships — are better than others. Sometimes you make decisions that make money, reduce waste or create customer delight worth over $1MM. I've never met a manager who said, "Yeah, I've got all the resources required to excel. I'm all set with adequate time, people, technology, rewards, clear outcomes and metrics..." Yet somehow managers swallow their frustrations. Somehow managers fight against ambiguity. How do managers like you succeed? You assess risks. You make smart choices. You adopt validated processes that work. This book is written for frustrated managers **who need to achieve outcomes and measure results.**

When I ask audiences, "How many of you are managers?" over 60% of those in attendance raise their hands. But when I ask, "How many of you are leaders?" only 30% raise their hands. Leaders are courageous and careful. Sometimes you raise your hand. Sometimes you sit on your hands. By definition, leaders influence the behavior of others toward a better future. Leaders tell stories from the front of the room. Leaders share public optimism. Do you collect data and anecdotes? Do you assess and recommend? Do you sell and deliver? Do you design and build? Then, do you step back to reflect? Sometimes leaders ask, "Now what?" They think about What's In It For Others, or WIIFO. This book is written for leaders like you **who need to influence the attitude and behavior of others.**

This **Objectives + Key Results (OKR) Leadership** book answers that "What's next?" question with a validated process that you can implement immediately. Simply put, **OKR Leadership is a process that enables managers and leaders to practice what matters.** OKR Leadership can help you and your team win by achieving objectives faster, at lower cost, with less waste. It's fairly easy to describe the OKR process, because it is an open source but deceptively simple process.[1] Definitions and examples of OKR Leadership are in the following paragraphs.

> OKR Leadership is defined as a process for managers and leaders to practice what matters.

This book is written for leaders and practitioners in **any-sized organization** (e.g., public or private, new or existing, small or large), in **any sector** (e.g., business, education, family, government, religion, career) in **any geography**.

This book contains countless examples from my consulting practice, since 1997, with over 10,000 leaders. Examples help people create meaning. About 80% of these examples apply to business and family leaders, and 20% apply to personal or individual leaders. OKR Leadership is practiced at the individual, team and organizational levels.

My primary objective is to provoke you into practicing OKR Leadership immediately. I often say, "Action leads to learning."

So, let's get started.

CHAPTER 1. INTRODUCTION

OKR Leadership in a small business

Over 70% of the U.S. economy is driven by small business leaders. Every small business owner struggles with people problems and resource problems. They need OKR Leadership.

George was the CEO and third generation family business owner of a $50MM retail business with 80 full time employees (FTEs). His primary objective was to accelerate succession planning for the next generation of family business leaders. In his words, "I don't want to screw things up."

At a management meeting I observed that the managers did not describe their business using any metrics. I asked George, "Where are the metrics that these managers are using to drive their business?" He sighed with fatigue, like so many business managers and leaders.

Then George hung his head in frustration.

I provided OKR definitions and templates and a free course on OKR Leadership skills to the managers (see www.action-learning.com for details). Then I worked individually with two key managers.

One manager's objective was to increase profit margins by 6% year over year. His first key result (KR) was to identify current measures for sales, expenses, overhead and profit within 30 days. His second KR was to distribute a one-page business summary to all other managers within 40 days. His third KR3 was to track and reward increased profit margins within 60 days. The result of his OKR Leadership was that he modeled accountability, transparency and business results for his team and the other four managers within 60 days. His department flourished and his career path was clear. Last month he reported the best revenue quarter in company history, and George smiled.

Sadly, the other 4 managers in their 75-year old small business were not willing to practice OKR Leadership. I encouraged George to hire one of his sons as a Director of Operations. He developed standards to drive consistency in training, job descriptions and product inventories. He also required all managers to provide OKRs. Those managers resisted change. One manager was encouraged to retire because his sales numbers were low. One manager was fired because he was unwilling to adapt to change. The other two passively resisted change as long as they could, then they were forced to practice OKR Leadership.

The point? OKR Leadership requires executive support from the business owner, George, and consistent practice from managers and leaders.

You can practice OKR Leadership in your career, team or organization today.

Definitions

OKRs are defined as a **management methodology that helps people focus activity on the same important issues throughout an organization.**[2] OKRs are a decision-making tool that can accelerate accountability and transparency. Typically, OKRs are voluntarily written by people at any level in an organization, and then shared "up, down and over." Managers cannot write OKRs for their direct reports. When people at each level of an organization write and distribute their own OKRs, then they are acting like CEOs or CHROs. They are able to truly "own their business."

OKRs are the secret sauce that drives the largest migration of financial assets and technological innovation ever recorded in human history to Silicon Valley, California since the 1970s.[3] As such, **OKR Leadership — a process for managers and leaders to practice what matters** – is the secret sauce that drives transformational leadership, employee engagement and the next generation of management consulting.

We can **define objectives as "what you do"**— qualitative statements that describe both operational and aspirational needs. Objectives are not written from the top-down or bottom-up in any organization. Each person on your team, and in your organization, must write their own objectives. Examples of good objectives include "Our team needs to increase new sales revenue 5%" or "We need to save at least $15,000 for our next family vacation." Examples of sloppy objectives include "Our team needs to make more sales" or "Our family really wants to go on a vacation trip."

Objectives are defined as qualitative statements
that describe what you must do
to meet or exceed your goals.

Business psychologists like me know that objectives can increase agency (individual choice), employee engagement, desired retention, measurable innovation, and drive organizational transformation. For example, one objective for this book is to provide the essential tools for managers or practitioners like you to lead your organizations. A second objective for this book is to provide examples of how to identify risks or blind spots, and solutions for any individual, team or organization to win.

Key Results (KRs) are defined as "how you measure that objective." KRs are quantitative statements. They answer the formula "as measured by" or "from X to Y by Z date." An example is, "We will track gross revenue quarterly and reward new sales with a 1% commission incentive in Q2."

> Key Results (KRs) are defined as 3-5 quantitative
> statements that answer the formula
> "as measured by" or "from X to Y by Z date."

In organizational leadership, KRs metrics drive desired objectives over time. Managers and leaders who apply OKRs to their organizations can accelerate outcomes in less than 12 months. To show you more specifically *how to practice OKR Leadership*, this book contains dozens of OKR Leadership examples from my clients in large and small organizations. One example of a KR for this book is to provide at least eight validated examples in each chapter.

By definition, an **organization** is any group of two or more people. When you and your partner or loved one work together, then you are in an organization of two people. When you and others work together, even if it is a messy process, then you are in an organization.

A **team** is any group of two or more people with a shared objective or scorecard. Teams are often described by their characteristics (e.g., virtual, direct, cross functional, ad-hoc, informal, and so on). For example, when golfing in a scramble tournament, your direct team of 4 players shares the objective of beating all other teams in the competition. All 4 players hit the drive, then you take the best ball and play from there. All team members share the same objective: to hit the ball into the cup with fewer strokes than players on any other team. Each team member keeps the score using mutually agreed rules.

But teams only win when they share objectives and leverage individual talents.

And because that is such a rarity, most teams fail.

Challenges

Implementing OKR Leadership is a challenging process for at least three reasons. People resist change. People are aspirational and often confused. People require choices.

People resist change because no one, ever, wants to be controlled or changed. This is evident with any child who breaks a rule, or any adult who breaks a law. Ask anyone who is managed by a ruthless manager, or anyone required to read this book. Historians have documented countless examples of resistance to change — from the last merger and acquisition, to the first known acts of stealing or slavery. Understanding this resistance matters; it needs to be considered. For that reason, this book contains examples of how you can manage conflict, accelerate your career, and create meaning using new research in psychology. People will always resist being asked – or forced – to make changes. But OKR Leadership can provide choice (agency) for that universal tendency to resist change.

Second, people are aspirational and often confused. We get distracted. We stop — then start — then start something else. All humans aspire to create a better world. Ask any parent of a new-born child about their dreams for that child. Ask any business creator. Ask any team about their capacity to win, or any leader with hopes for his or her team. But how do you know if you are climbing the best mountain or pursuing the best objectives? We get confused. We require feedback and client validation. Our aspirations matter; they define us as individuals and drive innovation. Thankfully, people like you aspire to make big dents in the world. Teams increase your probability of making those dents even bigger. This book is filled with practical examples of how people reduce confusion, and how teams can win. It will show you how OKR Leadership can accelerate your team and create competitive advantages.

Third, people change when they voluntarily *choose* to act, not when someone forces them to accept a sales quota. Top-down hierarchical leadership models often reduce risk taking. Ask anyone who blames others, or who hates their manager. The ability to make a choice matters. People flourish when they choose to create positive emotions, better relationships, deeper engagement, meaningful accomplishments, and purpose in their lives. The good news is that more people are flourishing today than ever in recorded history.[4] This book is filled with examples of new research in applied psychology that describes what those people are choosing to do, and what you can do.[5] Implementing OKR Leadership *requires* that people make individual choices and find meaning. It will allow you and your team to flourish in this same way.

Implementing OKR Leadership requires that you master two levels: 1) How OKR Leadership works for me, WIIFM or What's In It For Me, and 2) How you can implement OKR Leadership in your team, WIIFO or What's In It For Others. Leaders need to practice leadership. You need to look in the mirror and also look over the fence.

> The primary objective of this Objectives + Key Results (OKR) Leadership book is to provoke you and your team to practice leadership.

Assumptions for this book

1. **Leaders must practice leadership, just as physicians practice medicine or attorneys practice law.** Ask any leader with a critical deadline or product launch or fear of losing their job... urgency requires leaders to know what works. Leaders must take action; they must assess and recommend because it is critical for humanity.

2. **Action leads to learning.** Like any feedback loop, if your loved one states "Honey, we need to talk", then you stop to listen. All humans aspire to create a better future for ourselves and our loved ones.

3. **You are capable of practicing OKR Leadership today.** Nothing is holding you back. This book is a practical guidebook designed for you to accelerate your individual or team outcomes. You, dear reader, can do the work of practicing OKR Leadership *immediately.*

Why this book title?

Books with the word "Leadership" in the title outsell "management" books because few readers aspire to be managers. Yet every time I ask audiences, they confirm that they aspire to be leaders. This book is written for any reader or manager, at any level of your organization, who practices leadership. But of course, that doesn't tell the whole story.

When I stroll through an airport bookstore, I notice the number of business books with expletives in the title. They are provocative. I understand that rage and emotional appeal may increase book sales, but I have no desire to be associated with such titles. The title "Leadership Matters" may be a declarative book title that reflects today's zeitgeist – but that title lacks impact, and some description.

In March 2019, I was asked to speak at the Metrics That Matter (MTM) Symposium, filled with 150 delightfully nerdy people who spend their days applying metrics to business outcomes. The subtitle of the conference was "Building Your Impact Story." Business impact examples included Mastercard, Aon, BP, Cisco, and TELUS.

My presentation was called "Measuring the effectiveness of coaching programs." I shared with the group that formal learning programs, such as instructor-led classes, are being displaced by self-directed adult learning and individualized coaching programs. Market demands shift like the weather or your favorite social media trending topics. A book with the title "Leadership Matters" may be a respectful nod to the MTM consultants and the MWM book, but that title is not very provocative either.

To that end, this book title, "Objectives + Key Results (OKR) Leadership; How to apply Silicon Valley's secret sauce to your career, team or organization," represents the urgent market demand for practical outcome-based solutions that managers, leaders and practitioners like you can apply immediately.

Why this book design?

This book combines fictional dialogues with nonfiction explanations in each chapter because that's how our brains process data. Fiction defines our values and helps us create meaning. But we also create meaning with nonfiction.

I studied and taught literature for 13 years, because readers need stories to entertain and teach values like empathy. There are superb leadership lessons from fictional characters such as Hamlet, Celie, Odysseus or Hermione Granger. Then I studied and taught business psychology and management consulting for 21 years, because leaders drive organizational change. Nonfiction enables leaders to assess data and recommend actions. Just as each reader will process the same sentence in different ways, each chapter in this book contains fictional dialogs and nonfictional explanations designed to provoke you to practice OKR Leadership.

Each chapter is also designed to allow managers or academics or book groups to use this book's content as an independent activity. A chapter could be the text for your case study or your training program. Some readers may want to skip sections, like the fictional dialogues.

Others may want to skip the summary of key points. Like any practical guidebook, this book is designed for readers to take what you need and skim the other content.

Each chapter typically contains these four sections:

a. Key points, assumptions and definitions
b. Fictional interactions
c. Nonfictional explanations, validated practices, figures
d. Summary of key points, central questions

The final chapter contains endnotes, glossary and a quiz, references, definitions, and digital resources for you and your team to practice OKR Leadership.

OKR Leadership examples

When I lead workshops, I often say that leaders practice leadership, just as physicians practice medicine and attorneys practice law. In other words, *all* professionals describe their practice. So, think about it: do you practice leadership?

Consider the following examples from two very different organizations.

OKR Leadership in a F500 organization

The first example highlights the process of practicing OKR Leadership in a large organization. One of my clients wanted to build a culture of fiscal accountability using objectives and key results. The president, Nathan, was an executive coaching client leading a $5B industry with over 8,000 full-time employees (FTEs) in North America. In only 20 years, their company had grown from acquisitions — resulting in silos of information and fiscal practices that required centralization. Nathan had read about OKRs, shared some objectives with his direct reports, and wanted to accelerate their adoption. In Q418, I delivered a 2-day leadership training program for his senior leadership team of 60 Regional Vice Presidents, Vice Presidents, and General Managers. In Q119 all participants in that program developed their OKRs and monitored their progress in team coaching calls with my associates.

In Q219, at the Leadership Summit with 700+ leaders in the audience, Nathan shared examples of his personal and professional OKRs. He stated, "As long as I'm in this role, we will adopt OKRs to drive fiscal accountability in our organization." Executive sponsorship requires that leaders practice this kind of example-setting. After Nathan shared the state of the business, I led a 90-minute keynote session with some of the following content. Then I provided training workshops so that they could share OKR Leadership practices "up, down and over within their organization."

These leaders quickly became frustrated; they realized that they needed to crawl and walk before they could run. They said things like, "We know what Nathan wants, but we don't know *what* objectives are critical for *our* business," or, "We are all using different data collection formats, from excel to power point to photos. We need to invest in an OKR software solution." They wanted their managers to tell them what to do. But OKRs *cannot be cascaded* by others; they *must be written* by each person.

When I reviewed the over 300 OKRs submitted onto a SharePoint site, they ranged from vague items like "salespeople rebuilding" and "leadership development" to the ridiculous "smile more when I see my manager." (Truly. I can't make up this example.) Over the next 6 months, I provided 15 direct and virtual training programs to over 1,500 associates. I reviewed countless OKRs with senior leaders. The corporate university team created short instructional videos. They needed more education, but they also needed to *practice* OKR Leadership.

The results were uneven in year one. A corporate team found a $1MM savings within 6 months, because they could minimize expenses from vendors. One regional team found expense reductions in one product line that they could replicate in other products. One district team increased employee engagement scores over 15% within 6 months by increasing stay interviews (regular engagement conversations) from 40% to over 63%. One manufacturing team tried a new process and decreased costs over 300% in 30 days. Other teams are still struggling to apply OKR Leadership. The president, Nathan, recently said, "We are pushing boulders uphill. Fiscal accountability takes time. But we are showing measurable improvements every quarter."

You may be wondering why I shared an example that doesn't depict complete success. But it shows that OKR Leadership requires practice. You can apply OKRs in your large organization today, knowing that some will take time to take hold.

OKR Leadership in a family

OKRs aren't just for business. It's entirely possible to apply OKR Leadership within a family. Perhaps you have had the opportunity to teach someone how to drive a car. Many of us know that when the objective is to teach your child how to drive a car, the experience can be terrifying.

Imagine the scene: your objective is to teach enough basic skills so that your loved one can drive away safely. You start by teaching safety protocols like "wear your seat belt" and "always keep two hands on the steering wheel at "9 and 3." You explain the functions of the gas pedal, brake pedal, gears and all those shiny buttons on the dashboard. Then you offer encouragement as your loved one shifts into gear and drives from 0 to 30 mph within a mile. Your key results (KRs) often follow that formula "from x to y by date."

I myself have two children. One child drove from 0 to 30 mph within a mile. That caution led to a career mitigating risk in insurance. Our other child drove from 0 to 30 mph within 100 yards. That aggression led to a career in sales.

You can see how OKRs might work when used within the confines of a family. Like any team, family members typically struggle with communication and conflict. In the example above, I tried to communicate my expectations for safety, and to coach our children to avoid conflict. I used the AD-FIT™ coaching model (which we'll go into more detail on in chapter 4) to help our children assess their strengths and define their objectives. Like most managers, most parents struggle for a globally validated coaching model. The reason I trademarked the AD-FIT™ coaching model was because my clients kept asking, "What works?" On good days, I am an effective family leader.

The point of this example? You can apply OKR Leadership in your family today.

Now that we've gone through some real-life scenarios, let's consider a fictional (but realistic) one. How familiar is the following dialog to you and your team?

Fictional dialog

Scene: Breakfast meeting with friends, anywhere, current time.

Alice: I'm so frustrated. My manager just announced that the project we've been working on for the last 2 months is "no longer important."

John: What?! I thought your team was mission critical. You've been recognized as one of the best managers in your organization. What's going on?

Alice: I have no idea. Pete took today off because he is so upset. He's been a flight risk for months. Both Nickee and Eduardo looked like they were sucker punched at the end of the day yesterday. I don't know how to help them. I tried to ask my manager why the project was killed.

Karl: You've talked about your frustrations with him before. And your frustrations with your organization.

Alice: Yes... I do dump on you in these breakfast meetings. We recently lost a big client. We had some negative press after that scandal last quarter. We rarely meet revenue projections. We have low engagement scores. And now my team is totally frustrated. I think I need to find another job.

John: Well, we've talked about how objectives and key results have helped people at my organization. You've heard me rave about our transformation in the last year.

Alice: Yes. You've talked all about how OKRs have been the "secret sauce" in Silicon Valley over the last 50 years, and how it helps managers and the people who report to them make smarter decisions.

Karl: That's ridiculous. I don't think there are any secret sauces in business. Rome wasn't built in a day, and neither was Silicon Valley. This idea that the workforce is changing is greatly exaggerated.

John: I agree with you, Karl. We live in an age of social media hype and inflated claims. I think of OKRs as a management approach that works well with knowledge workers in technology organizations. No question about the impact there. And I think OKR Leadership is a bigger topic.

Karl: Huh? You mean there is a bigger flag on a bigger flagpole?

John: Yes. OKR Leadership is an outcome-based process that can help teams win. You can learn OKR Leadership. Leaders influence others' behavior toward a better future. A process like OKRs can help managers track behaviors. Individuals can accelerate their careers or make more money. Teams can make smarter decisions that increase efficiency, or effectiveness, or achieve outcomes. Individual and team leadership matters.

Alice: Hmm. I guess I need to learn more about OKR Leadership. I need to know what really works.

Question: Which of these characters reflects what you are currently thinking about OKR Leadership?

Figure 1 summarizes some key facts. The complete OKR Leadership Fact Sheet is described in chapter 8.

Figure 1: OKR Leadership Facts

Objectives = What is to be achieved. They are qualitative, subjective, and significant.

Key Results (KRs) = 3-5 quantitative measures that verify the status of any objective with numbers.

OKR Leadership = A process for managers and leaders to practice what matters.

OKR Leadership is:

1. Radical for top-down hierarchical organizations to implement
2. A bridge between silos (e.g., operations and human resources, regional and corporate) that need to share resources or collaborate
3. Individually written by people at any level of a team or organization

OKR Leadership is NOT:

1. Tied to performance reviews, compensation or rewards
2. A new fad or unvalidated approach to decision-making
3. A "silver bullet" for every career, team or organization

A short history of OKR Leadership

Historians and psychologists study how we create meaning using our mental maps or rose-colored glasses. Want a quick example? Consider, for instance, how you respond to these four short phrases:

- o Social networks.
- o Power and influence.
- o Feminist.
- o Functional perspective.

You read the phrase, then you created meaning. Right? For over 4,500 years of recorded history, people have always created their own meanings when describing organizations.

Here's another example. How do you complete this sentence: "In the beginning..."?

Your answer to this creation story question probably includes some hierarchy of social order. For instance, God created man. Men had power over women. Nobility had power over slaves. Property owners had power over workers. The golden rule was clearly understood: those with the gold ruled over others. Just as you created meaning when you answered the creation story question, people throughout history have always created social order.[6]

The field of psychology can be described as a subject with a long past but only a short history. The "long past" explored ancient questions such as "What makes life meaningful?" or "How can I provide a better life for my children?" The short history of psychology as a formal discipline is only about 100 years old, and the even shorter history of positive psychology is only about 20 years old. Positive psychology is defined as the scientific study of well-being and optimal human functioning.[7] As a social science, most psychologists explored how people respond to adverse stimuli (e.g., war, disease, anxiety or depression). Then, in 1998, the American Psychological Association, led by Martin Seligman and others, reversed direction to explore new research questions such as "How do people flourish?" and "What can leaders do to create competitive advantages in organizations?" Today, applied psychologists pragmatically ask, "What really works?"

The "Father of OKRs" title is attributed to Andy Grove, the founder and CEO of Intel. Andy literally wrote the textbook on semiconductors in 1967, well before Silicon Valley, California attracted the largest migration of financial and technical assets in human history. Andy also wrote *"Only The Paranoid Survive"* in 1996, as a reminder of market volatility and the need to measure business details. His father was killed at Auschwitz, Germany, and he fled Nazism with his mother at age 20. Andy was trained as an engineer. He wanted to design processes that maximize productivity and innovation.

American inventor and venture capitalist John Doerr worked for Andy Grove. John wanted to learn how to implement OKRs at technology companies, and in other sectors. Then in 1999, John made an $11.8M investment in 12% of Google when working at Kleiner-Perkins. The co-founders of Google wanted to organize data globally. When John introduced OKRs to Google, co-founder Larry Page said, "Well, we need to adopt some management approach." The rest is history. I strongly recommend John Doerr's best- selling book, *Measure What Matters*, (2018) for a dozen examples that range from the Gates Foundation to Bono.[8] Today, Google incorporates OKR leadership into all global decision-making. And Google is a $9 Billion company in 2018. Today, there are countless organizations implementing OKR Leadership.

By June, 2019, only 6 months after its publication, *Measure What Matters* had monthly book sales that exceeded $40,000. As described in Google Trends, searches for "OKR examples" increased from 0 in 2013 to over one hundred per day in December 2018 to coincide with the publication of that best seller.

Clearly, those book sales and search trends and organizations suggest a ready marketplace for validated processes that describe the secret sauce in Silicon Valley and management consulting.

The next three chapters discuss the "what, why and how" of OKR Leadership. Chapter five is designed for anyone in career transition. Chapter six is for anyone in a family or a family-owned business. Chapter seven is for trends and practicing OKR Leadership. Chapter eight is for resources.

So, let's get started.

Key points from chapter 1

1. **Objectives and Key Results (OKRs)** is a management methodology that helps people focus activity on the same important issues throughout their organization.
2. **Objectives** describe what you want to do. They are qualitative and subjective. Examples of objectives include "Increase revenue" or "Reduce undesired turnover."
3. **Key Results (KRs)** are the measures of each objective. They are quantitative and measurable. Examples include "increase recurring client sales revenue from \$500K/month to \$525K/month by the end of Q3" or "increase 1:1 performance reviews by 8% at all warehouses within 30 days."
4. **Leadership** is defined as influencing others' behavior toward a better future. The primary skill of effective leaders is public optimism.
5. Leaders practice leadership because it is challenging and critical for humanity.
6. People are both aspirational and confused.
7. You are capable of practicing OKR Leadership today.

Key questions from chapter 1

1. What is one objective for your career, team or organization?
2. What are 3-4 key results that you could use to measure that objective?
3. How could OKR Leadership address the problems your organization is facing?
4. What could be the ultimate goal of practicing OKR Leadership in your organization?
5. How could implementing OKR Leadership benefit you or your loved ones?

CHAPTER 2. WHAT IS OKR LEADERSHIP?

Fictional dialog

The scene: After work hours with drinks, any location, present day.

John: Are you kidding me? How can you ignore a multi-trillion-dollar story? There is no simple explanation for the biggest migration of financial assets into one small corner of one state in one country in the last 40 years.

Karl: Huh? What are you talking about?

John: Go back in time to 1988. Imagine telling your grandfather that there will be over 2,500 new companies created in the farmlands near San Jose, California within 40 years. There will be more billionaires per capita there than anywhere on earth, and that over 35% of the F500 companies will be startups without revenue histories. Imagine telling him that those new companies don't even exist yet.

Alice: And may *not* exist 20 years from now...

Enrique: Right. Because their billion-dollar market valuations are absurdly inflated.

John: Maybe. Back to the question. What would your grandfather say?

Enrique: He wouldn't say anything. My grandfather never had the means to invest in any companies.

Alice: My grandfather didn't have much money either. But he always had *opinions* on investing. He would probably say, "Run away!" You are describing a ridiculous market. He would say, "Only the paranoid survive." Right?

Karl: My grandfather had money to invest. He would say, "Show me the numbers." Then he would study the business costs and benefits with his cronies. I suppose that if it made sense for him to invest, then he would want to meet the leadership team.

John: Exactly. That's what investors have always said: Show me the numbers. Assess and recommend. Doesn't the Silicon Valley story make you a little curious about their secret sauce? You know, the "black box" that led to transformational changes *there*, instead of Chicago or Houston?

Alice: Hold on John, there may not be a black box. We know that federal investments in technology after the world wars led to the internet and space technology. We know that ties to elite universities like Stanford and Berkley were designed to provide free labor and a ready-to-hire marketplace for software engineers.

Enrique: Exactly. And local towns like Mountain View, California, provided generous tax incentives to build companies in their back yards. New funding approaches like venture capital was piloted in California because investors didn't want the conservative investment approaches from Wall Street.

John: All true. Many critical factors were necessary—but not sufficient.

Karl: Huh? Don't get nerdy on us. What do you mean?

John: What else occurred in the 1970s that redefined how people work? (*silence*). There were social protests and Vietnam. The top-down structural models that managers had imposed throughout history no longer worked. Those liberal non-conformist technology workers wanted freedom to develop their own solutions. They wanted to collaborate with anyone from any social network or ethnicity. They demanded open access to information so that they could make informed decisions.

Enrique: I'm picking up what you're laying down. It reminds me of that quote, "Never doubt that small teams of committed people will change the world. They have always done so." Margaret Mead was an anthropologist who made that point. But it's true for Bill Gates, Steve Jobs and every financial leader in the business biography section of the Barnes and Nobles bookstore.

John: Yes. The main point is that small teams of people need to know what to concentrate on. Like a goal post or milestone or deployment. They need a little bit of structure to focus their activities.

Alice: Right. And a productivity measure with a number and a date. We have that now on my team. Get x done by June 15, or whatever date.

Karl: I understand that. We all need a simple tracking system. Something that anyone can access to see what I'm working on, what you're working on. Maybe to explore who has expertise in some aspect of my current work... someone who can be a resource for me... hmmm.

Alice: That's good for you, Karl, because you're so self-directed. But I don't see how a simple tracking system could work with someone like Leroy, on my team. He's a follower who always seems to be four steps behind the rest of my team.

Enrique: Yeah, I was just thinking of another slacker on *my* team.

John: Let's flip the slacker example around. Who should be tracking productivity for the slackers on your teams? A manager? It's possible that the "Leroys" in the workplace may have the best intentions but don't know what to focus on. Do a little risk analysis here... What if one process reduced the individual variability in the team? For instance, what if Leroy had to declare his outcomes, what he wanted to work on? And what if Leroy's outcomes had to relate to his boss' outcomes so that there was a clearly defined business need for that outcome?

Alice: You mean like SMART goals or KPIs?

John: Not quite. Those are top-down models typically written by managers. They don't motivate individuals to think collaboratively or innovate. In fact, they *de*-motivate most knowledge workers and professionals.

Karl: Yeah. I can attest to that. I left three companies because managers tried to tell me what to do. And they never paid me what they promised.

John: I suppose we all have those stories. But let's return to the Leroy example. That poor guy can't defend himself because he's not drinking with us now. But he is representative of thousands of people. What if Leroy's manager tasked him with stating his outcomes and key results, his OKRs, on an accountability software platform that was distributed throughout the company? And what if his manager reviewed Leroy's OKRs monthly or quarterly to give him feedback on what to focus on, and how to measure his productivity?

Alice: I imagine that Leroy would do more productive work. Others would know what he was working on. There would be more accountability all around.

Enrique: Right. So when Leroy completed a significant OKR, then he would get rewarded. With public recognition. Or a spot bonus.

John: Exactly. The main idea behind OKRs is that they accelerate accountability and transparency. They provide a structure for flatter organizations to validate customer feedback and iterate new solutions.

Karl: I'm still confused. Maybe I need another drink. Or a walk. So the secret sauce to innovation in Silicon Valley is what, exactly?

John: The secret sauce is how leaders practice leadership. Specifically, when leaders and managers adopt the OKR Leadership process, then workers can transform organizations and create new markets.

Alice: You know, I don't think this story is unique to Silicon Valley. My aunt is running a church in Minnesota that seems to have a similar approach to managing others.

Enrique: Yeah, I think you're right, Alice. I know someone running a small business in Denver that seems to be applying this OKR methodology. I'm on their advisory board and they post financial updates to me every month.

Karl: Hmmm, so maybe this OKR discussion is a bigger conversation about social change and agency for workers?

John: Now *you* sound nerdy, Karl. But I think you're right. Maybe we should each contribute to a book on how OKR Leadership matters in different sectors or different organizations...

Question: Which of these characters reflects what you are currently thinking about OKR Leadership?

What is OKR Leadership?

As stated in chapter one, almost every sport you play has a scoreboard, or a finish line. When you drive your car, you stay between the lines to reach a goal. When you manage others, you always maximize their productivity. When you manage a business you always measure what matters... right? Well, not always.

> OKR Leadership is a process for managers
> to practice leading what matters.

Objectives

This chapter starts by defining objectives in some detail. Objectives describe what you want to do. They are qualitative and subjective. Examples of good objectives include:

- We want to win the Super Bowl
- We want to drive to Chicago
- We want to grow our revenue
- We want to increase profit margins
- We want to put a man on the moon by the end of the decade

TIPS: Write 3-4 objectives at most, then focus on only ONE most important objective for your business outcomes. Each person must write their own OKRs because each person manages their own business outcomes.

There are two types of objectives: operational and aspirational. Operational objectives are the important activities to *maintain* your business, whereas aspirational objectives are the important activities to *transform* your business. You want to strive for 60% aspirational objectives in your team – and you want to reward aspirational OKRs that are not achieved within a quarter. (Chapter 4 will go into more detail on this.)

> There are two types of objectives:
> operational objectives and aspirational objectives.

Activity

Practice writing objectives for your business using each of these headers:

Sales operational objective: _____

Sales aspirational objective: _____

People operational objective: _____

People aspirational objective: _____

Process operational objective: _____

Process aspirational objective: _____

Technology operational objective: _____

Technology aspirational objective: _____

Key Results

Key results (KRs) are 3-5 ways to measure each objective. They are quantitative and measurable. Examples of good KRs are:

- Our football offense will gain at least 300 yards per game
  We will drive for 7 hours a day until we arrive in Chicago
- We will track gross revenue quarterly and reward new sales with a 1% commission incentive in Q2
- We will reward each business unit with a 6% profit margin and a 2% reduction in expenses in Q4
- We will build a lunar module weighing under 40,000 pounds by December 1965

TIPS: Use numbers! Business leaders require numbers to drive accountability and transparency. You should have no more than 5 KRs for each objective. Too many KRs will cause you to lose your focus.

To simplify this chapter, here are two formulas worth adopting immediately.

KR Formula #1

Adopt the formula "as measured by" to confirm if something is a good OKR. "I will_(do this objective) as measured by_(these 3-4 KRs)."

If you cannot make that formula work, then you do not have a good OKR. *Yet.* Ask a colleague for feedback and edit your KRs until they can fit into Formula #1.

Good OKR example: We will win the Super Bowl as measured by 1) our offense will gain at least 300 yards per game, 2) our defense will give up less than 100 yards per game, and 3) our special teams will average a 25-yard punt return.

Bad OKR example: We will win the Super Bowl as measured by valiant efforts and loyal fans.

KR Formula #1: State "as measured by"

KR Formula #2: Adopt "from x to y by z date"

KR Formula #2

Adopt the formula "from x to y by z date" when writing KRs. It will force you to use numbers, and model transparency.

Good examples of KR Formula #2:

- We will develop our HR communication plan from 10% to 80% by Q419 to keep us aligned
- We will reduce scrap costs from x to y by Q4 to save at least $100k

- We will reduce SGA (general administrative overhead) by 200 basis points from x to 41% by Q3 to generate at least $3MM in additional EBITDA
- We will increase retention rates of desired employees from x to 85% by the end of Q2

TIPS: Use the OKR Worksheet below, or download it from the free OKR Leadership course described at www.action-learning.com. You can edit this worksheet for your organization, and use the two formulas described above. I often provide this simple worksheet at workshops as the only handout. Review your OKRs with 6-10 others to solicit feedback regularly.

Figure 2: OKR Worksheet

OKR Worksheet

Name:	
Position:	
Manager:	

Objective 1:		Feedback date:	Feedback date:	Feedback date:
KR1:				
KR2:				
KR3:				
KR4:				

Objective 2:				
KR1:				
KR2:				
KR3:				
KR4:				

Objective 3:				
KR1:				
KR2:				
KR3:				
KR4:				

©2019 www.Action-Learning.com

OKR Leadership examples at a team level

Imagine a global organization designed around one objective: "to create a culture of fiscal accountability using OKRs." The following KRs followed from that one objective. When my team of 5 consultants drafted the initial KRs, we asked the client for feedback. Then we conducted pre-program qualitative interviews with 35% of the participants. *Then* we conducted quantitative surveys with all 60 participants. Over time, the KRs evolved into the following.

KR1: 100% of senior leadership team will develop and distribute individual OKRs at leadership training event in Q4 2018

KR2: 100% of senior leadership team will participate in two 60-min team coaching calls in Q119 with accountability cohorts to reinforce OKR Leadership practices

KR3: at least 80% of individual OKRs will be achieved within 60 days

Remember, the two types of objectives: operational and aspirational. In this example, KR1 and KR2 are operational objectives. They should be completed 100% of the time as designed. KR3 is an aspirational objective. We do not expect that all aspirational KRs will be attained. If they are, then they are too easy.

TIP: ask 6-10 others for feedback to clarify your OKRs regularly.

OKR Leadership examples at an organizational level

The following two examples of objectives from the CEO and President at a Fortune 500 global organization written in Q418 reflect OKR Leadership well.

From the CEO's "Third Quarter Update" email: "On Thursday, we reported our financial results for the third quarter of 2018. Taken as a whole, we had a solid quarter showing some progress on the three key priorities that need to capture the focus of everyone's attention over the next several years:

1. Highly profitable organic revenue growth
2. Improved EBITDA margins
3. Enhanced cash flow by accelerating the conversion of profits in to cash"

From the President's "This Week's Wholesale Weekly Progress Report (WPR)" email: "If you look back to a few of my WPRs, as well as commentary from the CEO, you will remember the three key consistent themes that we've been saying we need to stay focused on for our company:

1. Grow revenue profitably — ensure revenue is growing along with the same or higher gross margin %
2. Increase operating leverage — grow expenses slower than revenue
3. Improve cash flow — one way is to get paid quicker on our AR"

What do you notice about these two examples?

How do these executive examples relate to OKR Leadership at your team or organization today?

Key points from Chapter two, What is OKR Leadership?

1. **OKR Leadership** is a process for managers and leaders to practice what matters.
2. **Objectives and key results (OKRs)** is a management methodology that helps companies focus effort on the same important issues throughout their organization
3. **Objectives** describe what you want to do. They are qualitative and subjective.
4. **Key results (KRs)** are the 3-5 measures of each objective. They are quantitative and measurable.
5. **KR Formula #1:** Adopt the formula "as measured by" to confirm if something is a good OKR.
6. **KR Formula #2:** Adopt the formula "from x to y by z date" when writing KRs. It will force you to use numbers, and model transparency.

Key questions from chapter 2, What is OKR Leadership?

1. Have all of your team members written their OKRs?
2. Have you distributed OKRs for your organization or team?
3. How are you implementing OKRs in your business? (e.g., decision-making, performance management, bonus rewards, career development, individual development plans, or talent assessments.)
4. How are you implementing OKRs in your productivity measures? (e.g., effectiveness, efficiency, behavior outcomes or performance outcomes.)

5. To what extent are you using OKRs to drive your business? To what extent do you think OKRs will drive your future business?
6. What OKR resources do you need to locate?
7. Add your questions here...

Now that you know what OKR Leadership is, the next chapter explains why you should use OKR Leadership in your team or organization.

CHAPTER 3. WHY DO I NEED TO USE OKR LEADERSHIP?

Fictional dialog

Enrique: I don't care *why* I should do something. I just want to see the input and output. Show me the results.

John: Makes sense to me. Maybe you don't need to read this chapter.

Karl: Or maybe he does. If you want to know the research, this chapter may be useful.

Alice: I just want to see the results. Show me how to be more efficient or more effective.

John: Many people need to know the nerdy reasons to justify OKR Leadership to their boss. Practicing OKR leadership is challenging.

Question: Which of these characters reflects what you are currently thinking about OKR Leadership?

The short answer to the question "Why do I need to use OKR Leadership?" is that **you do *not* need to use OKR Leadership if your business is exceeding all performance expectations.**

But that is a slim possibility for three reasons. The first is that businesses either grow with some competitive advantage or die based on negative feedback from customers. OKR Leadership can provide that competitive market advantage. The second reason to practice OKR Leadership is because people are hierarchical, aspirational and confused. The third reason is because people require feedback when learning.

Let's look more closely at each of these.

> You do not need to use OKR Leadership
> if your business is exceeding
> all performance expectations.

A competitive market advantage

Businesses either grow or die; there is nothing in the middle. In a free market, capitalistic world view you *have* to grow, or you will die. Recent studies of variability on all public stock markets, or all annual lists such as Fortune 500, Forbes or Inc 1000 confirm this fact. Why assume that your business will *not* die? All organisms and organizations die, at some point. Over 30% of the top 100 companies on the Wall Street Stock exchange today did not exist 20 years ago, and many of those new organizations have adopted OKRs into their decision-making culture. Your business should and will cease to exist one day – unless, of course, you change in response to customer feedback.

Below are four examples of how you can gain competitive advantage in your global marketplace. Your team can win if you adopt the advantages of ISO human capital standards, leadership trust index (LTI), follower trust index (FTI), and psychological capital (PsyCap).

ISO human capital standards

You might know that the International Organization for Standardization (ISO) standards have defined quality improvement and safety investments in countless organizations since they were first introduced in 1947. These worldwide proprietary, industrial and commercial standards have been adopted in 164 countries. When you turn a faucet you expect clean water, because of ISO 14000 environmental standards. When you buy a product on line you expect quality, because of ISO 9000 quality standards. What about when you hire someone?

We are in a globally competitive talent economy. Imagine if your organization measured human capital data that increased investor confidence or determined your talent investment decisions? What if you collected and distributed data on the following 23 human capital measures into these 9 categories?

1. Ethics (number and type of employee grievances filed; number and type of concluded disciplinary actions; percentage of employees who have completed training on compliance and ethics).
2. Costs (total workforce costs).
3. Workforce diversity (with respect to age, gender, disability, and "other indicators of diversity"; and diversity of leadership team).
4. Leadership ("leadership trust," to be determined by employee surveys).
5. Organizational safety, health, and well-being (lost time for injury; number of occupational accidents; number of people killed during work).
6. Productivity (EBIT/revenue/turnover/profit per employee; human capital ROI, or the ratio of income or revenue to human capital).
7. Recruitment, mobility, and turnover (average time to fill vacant positions; average time to fill critical business positions; percentage of positions filled internally; percentage of critical business positions filled internally; turnover rate).
8. Skills and capabilities (total development and training costs).

9. Workforce availability (number of employees; scalability from full-time and part-time equivalents).

I recommend that you ask the following two questions quarterly, if you desire to be competitive in today's talent economy.

1. If these 23 ISO human capital standards become requirements for competitive advantage at our organization, then how would they affect our organization?
2. Most organizations spend over 60% of working capital on people, and that expense is 100% manageable. How are we investing in people at our organization?

I predict that ISO Human Capital standards will redefine how managers and leaders and workers interact in the next decade. Consider your organization.

OKR Leadership at privately held organizations may use these ISO human capital standards for directional initiatives. Examples include assessing and replacing managers with high turnover ratios identified as "toxic managers," or investing in high growth teams that require training in OKR Leadership skills. I have been hired to assess and recommend such changes.

OKR Leadership at publicly held organizations can also use these ISO human capital standards for multi-directional initiatives. Examples may include initiatives designed to retain more diverse employees, eliminating bias in hiring, or retaining desired employees with external coaching and consulting. I have also been hired to assess and recommend such changes.

Almost all leaders and managers struggle to collect and analyze data. The C-suite leaders I meet with expect me to provide a one-page talent summary update. Typically, they scan it in seconds and then look up. We review the talent summary update. Then I ask, "What do you want to focus on today?" Fortunately, I've developed a system for making sense of that data, which I share in this book. Chapter 4 will provide more details on the AD-FIT™ coaching process. For now, let's look at a second way that you can gain competitive advantage.

Leadership Trust Index (LTI)

I predict that massive changes driven by ISO human capital standards will accelerate accountability, transparency and data-driven decision making. Just as ISO standards have defined global standards in safety and quality and financial compliance since 1947, they will soon provide standards in human capital. Leaders in Europe are implementing ISO standards in human capital today.

One example of these new standards is described by Steve Maxwell, President of the Human Capital Management Institute, who presented at the Center for Talent Reporting Annual Conference, February 21, 2019 in Dallas, TX. He stated that global companies will likely establish and post a Leadership Trust Index (LTI) with other business metrics (e.g., shareholder value) that will inform institutional investors, private investors and global business leaders. Companies with higher LTI scores will likely attract more money, have higher engagement scores, experience lower turnover of desired employees, encounter fewer legal/ ethical/ safety complaints, and have a higher EBIT (earnings before interest and taxes) per employee.

If you invest in any publicly traded companies, then you have probably listened to a quarterly earnings call that included presentations from the CEO, CFO and VP of Investor Relations. These individuals are tasked with consistently distributing critical information for investors, without revealing any confidential information.

I worked with the CFO and VP of investor relations at a F100 healthcare company. Every 17 minutes during a particular earnings call, they responded to questions from a new set of institutional investors who each asked variations of the same prying question. The gist of their question was, "What else can you tell me that I can share with our investors about your company?" This exhausting process was designed to comply with investor access requirements. A publicly measured LTI would help make this scenario much more productive by sharing talent initiatives, investments and returns.

Can you imagine the impact of a publicly measured Leadership Trust Index (LTI) for institutional investors on your organization? How about the impact of an LTI on your investment decisions?

Follower Trust Index (FTI)

In addition to LTI, I've also piloted something I call the Follower Trust Index (FTI) in my recent consulting work. FTI can be defined as the extent to which you think others in your organization trust you. By definition, leaders require followers. But we rarely measure followership. Both LTI and FTI are variables that can be measured by asking these two questions: To what extent do you trust the leaders in your organization (LTI)? And, to what extent do you think others in your organization trust *you* (FTI)? Here are several examples of my recent findings.

In a recent OKR Leadership workshop with a small business client and 14 participants I found these results.

Q1. To what extent do you trust the leaders in your organization (LTI)? Score = 83%

Q2. To what extent do you think others in your organization trust you (FTI)? Score = 85%

In a recent OKR Leadership workshop with a F500 client I also asked for text responses. These responses may be representative of your organization.

Q1. To what extent do you trust the leaders in your organization (LTI)?

- Sometimes what sounds good at the top or the vision of what could happen is not the reality at the ground level.
- We continue to hear what employees have to say but sometimes we don't listen.
- Sometimes we dismiss the feedback that our customers give us.
- I have a high amount of trust with my direct leaders.
- Our senior leadership is very engaged and transparent at all levels.

Q2. To what extent do you think others in your organization trust you (FTI)?

- For the most part I think those who work for me trust what I say and my vision, but because of the complexity of making changes that sometimes go badly, I lose some trust.
- I've made mistakes but receive great support from my direct reports and peers.
- Some decisions or policies driven down from the regional or district level are not popular to location level employees.

- Working with teams in many different locations brings contradictory opinions about how things should be handled.
- We all try to communicate clearly why a certain directive needs to be implemented.

Both quantitative and qualitative scores are included in this third example from an OKR Leadership workshop that I delivered in July, 2019 to a small business with 9 participants.

Q1. To what extent do you trust the leaders in your organization? (Leadership Trust Index, LTI) Score = 89%

Open text responses:

- I view [the owner] as the only leader and trust her business sense completely.
- I trust myself to make smart business decisions.

Q2. To what extent do you think others in your organization trust you? (Followership Trust Index, FTI) Score = 86%

Open text responses:

- I would hope I am trusted - if not, I do not imagine I'd be allowed to be independent.
- As a part time, outside consultant, I am often not as involved in the company as others.
- This is a difficult question. Could be improved.

When I ask managers and leaders how they measure followership, they rarely have high quality responses. Their self-ratings are inflated, and their open text responses often describe intentions instead of actual behaviors. Leaders must have followers, by definition. There is a significant need for research on how your potential followers actually behave.

> Ask these two questions:
>
> To what extent do you trust the leaders
> in your organization (LTI)?
>
> To what extent do you think others
> in your organization trust you (FTI)?

One compelling reason for adopting OKR Leadership is to increase the frequency of conversations with your potential followers about what they say and do to achieve desired objectives. Feedback leads to learning, and always leads to competitive advantage for your organization (we'll speak more about this in Chapter 4.)

Psychological Capital (PsyCap)

Let's continue this discussion of the competitive advantage of OKR Leadership with a provocative question: Are you wealthy?

Some people answer that question based on their financial assets (e.g., net worth, liquid assets, real estate, savings, fixed assets, earning potential). Some people answer that question based on what they know, their human capital (e.g., knowledge, skills, abilities, certifications, intellectual capacity). Still other people answer that question based on who they know (e.g., social network, friends, colleagues, family).

There is nothing wrong or right with any of these first three views of capital. They often add meaning to life. They define objectives, and careers. It's important to point out that these are *resource-based* views of capital. In short, they describe finite resources that will disappear at some point. At the risk of sounding morbid, the fact is that in the last years of my life, I expect to spend most of my assets on healthcare, I will forget what I have learned, and I will forget my loved ones. Odds are, the same will happen to most people.

In contrast, Psychological Capital (PsyCap) is defined as who you are becoming, as shown in the figure below.

Figure 3.1: A new view of capital

Psychological capital (PsyCap) can be defined as "who you are developing into." It is measured by hope, efficacy, resilience, optimism: the HERO-within acronym. Researchers now discuss the unlimited, developmental potential state of "the HERO within" individuals and teams. OKR leaders and practitioners can apply PsyCap research to teams immediately.

There is always a gap between what researchers know and what practitioners do (since it takes some time for them to catch up). The following findings should interest OKR leaders:

- PsyCap can be developed or learned in a web-based program in 90 minutes[1]
- People with higher PsyCap scores report higher sales, higher job satisfaction, higher engagement scores, and lower attrition[2]

- Several studies have found that PsyCap scores describe 71% of the variance in employee engagement scores and 65% of job satisfaction scores[3]

My global research found that PsyCap can provide a competitive market advantage to leaders.[4]

I recently led an OKR workshop with a small business team of 23 leaders. In the pre-workshop survey, I asked these four PsyCap questions about hope, efficacy, resilience and optimism. You can use these same questions to measure the impact of your OKR Leadership training programs. The numbers that come after indicate the percentage of people who agreed with the statement.

1. Hope. I believe that I have "the will and the way" to achieve my goals. Score = 94%
2. Efficacy. I feel confident that I know what I need to do to achieve my goals. Score = 78%
3. Resilience. I can get through difficult times or challenges. Score = 89%
4. Optimism. I am optimistic about what will happen to me in the future. Score = 86%

One result that came out of asking these four questions is that this client determined a new objective and a new KR. They realized that they needed to develop role clarity and process improvements so that they could increase their efficacy scores from 78% to at least 90% within 6 months.

PsyCap and Performance

For decades, human resource managers have implemented a silly 9-box forced ranking system to assess potential (y axis) and performance (x axis). The results are often demotivating and misused. How can any manager accurately assess the potential of a direct report? What happens when the direct report has a family illness, special project, or pregnancy? The subjectivity of the 9-box grid can be immediately eliminated if managers used two objective and dynamic variables, such as PsyCap (y axis) and performance (x axis).

The PsyCap dimensions of hope, efficacy, resilience and optimism can be objectively measured with a 12-question survey from self-reports or customer feedback.[5] Anyone can develop their PsyCap – and their performance — and the scores can be ranked from low to medium to high. Additionally, anyone can create a 9-box grid – but I prefer to simplify models. An alternative is to adopt the 4-box grid shown below in Figure 3.2.

TIP: Assess each member of your team. Place their names on this 4-quadrant model. Focus most of your resources and attention on the performers, with higher PsyCap and higher performance scores. Minimize your resources on those with lower PsyCap and performance scores, because they do not deserve your attention. They can be introduced to PsyCap scores. If they choose to increase hope, efficacy, resilience or optimism, then they may become performers in your organization. If they do not choose to increase their PsyCap, then they should be encouraged to work in a different organization.

Figure 3.2: PsyCap and Performance Grid

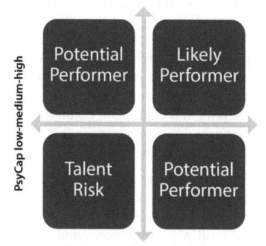

My experience is that when OKR leaders increase PsyCap, then they have a competitive advantage in business, education or families.[6] Most teams want to win. Your team can increase your competitive advantage if you embrace ISO human capital standards, leadership trust index (LTI), follower trust index (FTI), and psychological capital (PsyCap).

People are hierarchical, aspirational and confused

The second reason *why* you need to practice OKR Leadership is because people are hierarchical, aspirational and confused. Every organization aspires to improve the state of its members. Pick any organization in any culture — any social group or tribe. You create value and serve those in your social groups. You create order with some form of hierarchy; not because you require power over others, but because you strive for efficiency and effectiveness. Look for that hierarchy in any organization that you think is effective.

There is a pervasive myth that organizations are top-down, structured social constructs with organizational charts that cascade down in a pyramid. That top-down structure prevailed in the middle ages when members of the nobility controlled the distribution of food and protection in exchange for taxation or servitude. That structure was the dominant model in the industrial age, when productivity and capitalism defined global markets. However, that top-down structure has little value in today's information and networked age.

The dominant model today is a social network model that looks like a spider's web or a messy blob. Consider how you interacted with other people in the last 24 hours. You probably had multiple interactions, and each one provided some resources or information that you used to make decisions and achieve your objectives.

The dominant organizational model today is a network analysis model that looks like the messy blob image on the right side of Figure 3.3. Teams have evolved into a series of messy interactions with shared values, increased transparency, more access to information, and rewards based on influence.

Figure 3.3: How teams evolve

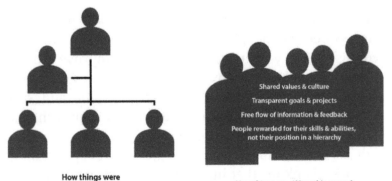

Shared values & culture
Transparent goals & projects
Free flow of information & feedback
People rewarded for their skills & abilities,
not their position in a hierarchy

How things were

How things are / How things work

(Image concept used with permission from Josh Bersin)

Consider how military units now work when attacked. Small direct teams of 4-8 people with specialized skills depend on technology from other virtual team members to complete their objectives. The U.S. military teaches warriors to "adapt and overcome" because nothing else works in battle. Ask any officer, or any veteran.

Consider as well how IBM uses social interaction and network analysis to track performance. They screen scrape all digital data to track individual and team behaviors. If you work at IBM and type, "I HATE MY BOSS!" into your company computer, then you should expect a quick response. The top 10 people who interact with an employee are the ones who provide the performance review feedback for that employee. And while the manager is one of those top 10 people, he or she is no more important than the other 9.

When I attended a Talent Analytics conference hosted by the Society of Industrial and Organizational Psychologists (SIOP) in October, 2016, I was astounded to learn the power of unstructured feedback and network analysis. Alan Wild, a VP at IBM, shared these findings:

- IBM measures employee engagement based on "real time" and unstructured data
- We can best help our managers and executives drive engagement by giving them data based on "real life" examples
- Engaging employees in design thinking improves engagement scores
- Managers are *not* the most important players in employee engagement; in fact,
- Employees are more influenced by their peers and colleagues than by their first line or second line manager

- A chronically disengaged peer has three times the negative impact of a highly engaged peer
- Chronically disengaged first line managers are toxic
- Nothing travels further and faster than a tweet containing bad news.

Do those findings surprise you?

Consider what *you* do when you have a professional (or even personal) problem. Typically, people seek information from 6-10 individuals before making a critical decision (e.g., to confront a difficult colleague, to initiate a big investment, to cancel a project after years of sunk costs.) And of course, you trust information from some people more than others. If you drew a chart of who you reached out to for information when you had a problem, it would look more like a spider's web or a messy blob than a hierarchical organizational chart. Now, think of what you do when you have a negative experience. Studies show that the average person typically complains to at least 7 people. And we rarely express gratitude for those who help us solve problems.

Consider the model for every social media platform. Facebook has likes and automated settings to distribute content to your friends. LinkedIn, Instagram, Twitter, Pinterest have followers and connections. Even retail sites like Amazon have product recommendations for "buyers like you" based on your viewing or shopping history. All organizations have a model or image that describes how people work. They may look like spiders webs, or messy blobs. Consider the playful images described in the next figure.

Figure 3.4: Organizational network charts

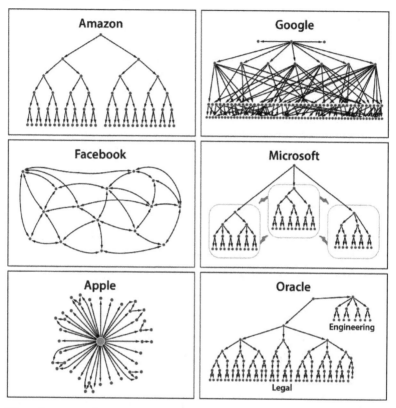

The fact is that most organizational charts today look more like spider's webs or messy blobs than anything linear. Silicon Valley technology companies and countless organizations have adopted OKR Leadership because they increase accountability and transparency.

However, you do not need to adopt OKRs in your organization. There are other options.

Consider the changes in management described in the next figure.

Figure 3.5: History of management consulting

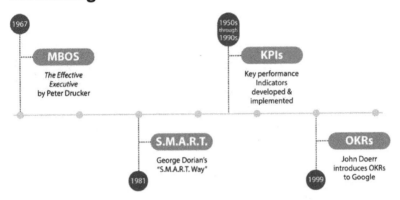

You might know that Management by Objectives (MBOs), SMART goals (Specific, Measurable, Attainable, Realistic, Time-bound) and Key Performance Indicators (KPIs) exist in organizations with static performance outcomes. And while they've been used for over 50 years (as the timeline indicates), they are all top-down hierarchies that do not work when collaboration, creativity and learning agility are required.

You may be wondering what the difference between OKRs and those other management consulting approaches even are. One difference is that OKRs *flatten the hierarchies* in most organizations so that people can do what matters. In *Measure What Matters (2018)*, John Doerr tells a story about flattening organizations by increasing the number of direct reports for each manager.

Psychologists have studied team effectiveness and determined that an average team size of 5-7 is more likely to be effective than a smaller or larger team. That's one reason why many managers have no more than 7 direct reports. But what is best for *your* organization?

Leaders at Google wanted to flatten their organization so that managers would have a minimum of 10 direct reports using OKRs, instead of having a maximum of 10 direct reports using some hierarchical structure. There is nothing inherently wrong with having only 5-7 direct reports. Unless, of course, your organization requires that you distribute information broadly to 10 or more direct reports using a process like OKRs to increase transparency and accountability.

How OKRs can work

Five ways that OKRs can work in your organization (adapted from Doerr, 2018) include their ability to help you:

1. **Align and connect for teamwork.** You establish transparent goals, connected to your company's top priorities.
2. **Track for accountability.** The work you do is driven by data. You hold periodic check-ins, engage in objective grading and continuous reassessment, and embrace no-judgement accountability.
3. **Stretch for amazing.** Employees are motivated to excel and test limits, and also have the freedom to fail, and to release ambition and creativity.
4. **Focus and commit to priorities.** You are very quickly able to identify what's important and what's not.
5. **Agency.** A subjective feeling of control, mastery, or purpose.

OKR Leadership increases agency

Another difference between OKRs and the other management consulting approaches described above is that OKR Leadership provides agency for individuals. Someone who has sense of agency or control feels a subjective awareness of controlling one's choices.

For instance, when a frontline supervisor named Tony writes his OKRs, he may be making choices for the first time in his working career. I recall walking with a 50-year old supervisor like Tony at a new nuclear construction project site with over 7,000 workers. The supervisor turned to me and said, "I've never been asked to write my objectives and key results before. I've always done what my manager told me I had to do to get her done in time and under budget. This is a new way of thinking about my team." This person is representative of thousands in today's workforce.

Statistically, over 50% of the employees in your organization are likely to be millennials, born between 1981-1996 in the U.S. As Pew Research data consistently report, these workers demand control – over their time, their work, and how those two things come together. (Chapter 6 will go into a more detailed explanation on the importance of agency in OKR Leadership and career development). Today, OKR Leadership provides an organizing structure for countless organizations.

How people are confused

This topic could be my next book title. There are many mis-used managerial practices that de-motivate people and reduce innovation. I've seen examples that managers and leaders in human resources should discard immediately including forced rankings, open 360 evaluations, annual pay for performance reviews, self-written reviews, hiring based on previous performance, mandatory supervisions and so-called "career ladders." If you want to see many more examples of confusion in leadership, see my book end notes[7]. The mere fact that I'm able to list so many examples shows that there is too much confusion about bad managerial practices.

But instead of discussing that confusion further, let me ask another provocative question. What do you consider more important for your executive presence: your identity (how you regard yourself) or your reputation (how others regard you)?

When I ask audiences this question, 50% state "identity." They state, "I have to know my strengths and weaknesses in order to be a strong leader." They argue that a positive attitude and high self-regard are critical variables in career development. They also claim that self-reports and personality assessments are valid indicators of executive presence.

The other 50% argue that reputation is more important, and believe that what others think defines their career. They state, "What others think about me is critically important. I'm always mindful of how to develop my reputation." They ignore self-reports and focus on team performance results or developing awareness of their blind spots.

> What is more important to you,
> your identity or your reputation?

Based on extensive research from Gallup, Pew Research, the Hogan assessment suite, my consulting work, and my global dissertation, here is a summary designed to reduce your confusion.

Identity is defined as *how I see myself.*

- Self-awareness is inflated and typically inaccurate (i.e., you may believe you have more self-awareness than you truly do, and what you believe is often not the full truth).
- Self-ratings of performance typically underestimate our capabilities (i.e., you are able to do more than you give yourself credit for).
- Identity is less predictive of your career success than feedback from others

Reputation is defined as *how others see me.*

- Other-awareness is variable and biased (i.e., others always have a different perspective that is biased and ever changing)
- Reputation is based on what others *think* I say or do, not what I *actually* say or do
- Reputation is more predictive of your future performance than your self-ratings

In short, most people are confused about the value of mandatory feedback, performance reviews, self-reports – things that require accurate feedback.

There are many reasons for the largest migration of financial and technological assets in human history to Silicon Valley, and OKR Leadership is one of the most compelling reasons for that migration.

OKR Leadership is also the secret sauce for management consulting because it increases agency for people, and agency determines all dimensions of flourishing (e.g., positive emotions, engagement, relationships, meaning and accomplishments, and the PERMA model – all of which we'll cover in more detail in Chapters 6 and 7.)

People require feedback when learning

The third reason why you should practice OKR Leadership is because people require feedback. We are social animals who want others to tell us when we're exhibiting desired behaviors, and be rewarded for those behaviors. We also require feedback when we exhibit undesired behaviors, in the form of penalties. We need this feedback to develop relationships, and to continue learning. Consider how quickly you make judgements about other people on social media, where outrageous statements are condoned.

Figure 3.6: People require feedback

Feedback determines the quality and quantity of our relationships. It's the way in which we interact with others to maximize their performance. It's how managers coach others, and how leaders influence others to follow. Feedback is how people learn desired behaviors.

The best feedback process for OKR Leadership is the AD-FIT™ process, which we'll cover next in chapter 4.

TIPS: Download and use the OKR Worksheet from chapter 2. Edit the worksheet for your team or organization.

Use the two KR formulas. Review your OKRs with 6-10 others regularly. Leaders require feedback.

Key points from chapter 3, Why use OKR Leadership?

1. OKR Leadership is a process for managers and leaders to practice what matters.
2. You do not need to use OKR Leadership if your business is exceeding all performance expectations (but odds are, it isn't).
3. Businesses either grow or die in response to customer feedback. There is nothing in the middle.
4. People are hierarchical, aspirational and confused. Every organization aspires to improve the state of its members.
5. People require feedback. Feedback is how managers and leaders interact with others to maximize their performance. The best feedback process for OKR Leadership is the AD-FIT™ process, which I'll describe in chapter 4.

Key questions from chapter 3, Why use OKR Leadership?

1. What are the top 3-4 OKRs that the executive leaders in your organization use?
2. How is your team or organization staying focused on your KR metrics (not milestones or tasks)?
3. How are you rationalizing your investment in OKR Leadership to your executives, champions, buyers, consumers, and clients?
4. Since practicing OKRs in your team or organization, what changes have you measured to date?

5. Since practicing OKRs in your team or organization, what new behavior or performance outcomes do you hope to measure?
6. Regarding the Leadership Trust Index (LTI): to what extent do you trust the leaders in your organization? (score from 1 low to 10 high) and why?
7. Regarding the Follower Trust Index (FTI): to what extent do you think others in your organization trust you? (score from 1 low to 10 high) and why?

Now that you know what OKR Leadership is and why you could use OKR Leadership in your team or organization, we'll delve into how to use OKR Leadership and introduce the AD-FIT™ coaching process in the next chapter.

CHAPTER 4. HOW DO I PRACTICE OKR LEADERSHIP?

If you are ready and able to practice OKR Leadership in your career, team or organization, then you are probably asking "*How* do I practice OKR Leadership?" That's why this is the longest chapter — because practicing OKR Leadership is challenging.

Like me, you may have listened to the award-winning "Car Talk" comedy show hosted on National Public Radio for 35 years. The hosts, "Click and Clack the Tappet Brothers" Ray and Tom Magliozzi, shared their contagious laughter. They also shared their wisdom on cars, people and relationships from the unlikely corner in Harvard Yard. They often talked about the "third half of the show, when some lucky listener would receive a special reward."

Feedback is that "third half" of the OKR Leadership process – and this chapter is the "third half" of this book because the AD-FIT™ process is the secret sauce of OKR Leadership. It will show you that can learn, teach, *and* practice OKR Leadership.

Question: Which of these characters reflects what you are currently thinking about OKR Leadership?

Fictional dialog

Karl: I met a sales director of a French company who said, "I never met my manager. He interviewed and hired me using Skype. I live near New York. I conduct sales throughout Central and South America. We never talk. In 18 months, I've never received any email or objectives from him."

Alice: Yikes. That's not even laissez-faire. That's an irresponsible manager.

Karl: Maybe. He was gone after 18 months. But the new guy is no different.

Enrique: So the norm at your company is to not provide *any* feedback? To let people swim or sink?

Karl: Yes. Very French.

John: My experience is that *all* people require feedback. But most don't know how to provide it. In fact, most people don't know anything about coaching others, and struggle to describe their future objectives. How else can we learn?

Alice: My experience is that people avoid feedback because they fear changing.

Karl: So, managers and leaders need to practice using a feedback protocol that leverages their strengths and objectives?

John: Yes. Daily. That sounds like the AD-FIT™ coaching process.

6 OKR Leadership practices

This chapter includes 6 OKR Leadership practices that you can implement immediately. They have been proven to work well.

1. Practice a growth mindset.
2. Practice asking great questions.
3. Practice sharing your OKRs.
4. Practice alignment.
5. Practice an accountability cadence.
6. Practice AD-FIT™ coaching.

Let's look at how to practice each of them in more detail.

1. Practice a growth mindset, not a fixed mindset

There are many topics that I do not understand, and I am not willing to understand. This is what I mean by having a "fixed mindset." For instance, I have a fixed mindset toward violent martial arts, because I do not understand how such violence can be a sport. I practice a fixed mindset toward opera, because I do not enjoy listening to dramatic sopranos. However, I practice a *growth* mindset toward learning, because curiosity is one of my strengths.

A growth mindset requires an attitude of curiosity. Practicing curiosity allows you to more easily listen to others, assess new data, and make better decisions. Managers and leaders who practice a growth mindset are more effective, and their

teams are more engaged and productive[1]. One of my favorite large studies found that CEOs who are "other-oriented" are five times more effective than CEOs who are self-oriented[2].

One way to foster a growth mindset is to ask questions like, "What can I learn?" or "How can I serve others?"

2. Practice asking great questions

Most people know that questions typically begin with the words "who, what, when, where, why or how." There are two types of questions: open-ended questions (e.g., begin with "what" or "how") or closed questions (e.g., begin with "who", "when", "where", or "why"). When you ask a closed question such as "When will you finish this project?" you will get a short answer (i.e., "tomorrow.") That closes the door to additional conversation. However, when you ask an open-ended question such as "What resources are critical for a prototype?" then you get a long answer—thereby opening the door for practicing OKR Leadership.

Some cultures and organizations do not promote open-ended questions. Some cultures value structure and order, like Nazi Germany (to take an extreme example) or Chinese technology companies (for another extreme example). In these situations, closed questions are the cultural norm. But in today's information age with open access to search engines for data in most countries, many managers and leaders can practice asking open-ended questions every hour of every day. As organizational development consultant Peter Drucker is attributed with saying, "The leader of the past knew how to tell; the leaders of the future will know how to ask."

Below is a short list of open-ended questions that you can use with your team. There are more open-ended questions at the end of every chapter in this book. Please edit these questions for your career, team or organization.

Efficiency questions

How are we measuring efficiency?

What can we do to improve measures of efficiency?

Effectiveness questions

How do we know that we are being effective?

What measures can we implement to be more effective this day/ week?

Outcome questions

How do we know that we are achieving the performance or behavior outcomes that our clients require?

What else can we do to achieve our performance or behavior outcomes?

I regularly pose the following question to many of my OKR Leadership clients. I strongly encourage you to adopt it and use it quarterly as a pulse survey, like Net Promoter Score: "To what extent are you using OKR Leadership to drive your business?" Score from 1 (low) to 10 (high). I use this OKR Pulse Survey question to measure adoption and organizational change over time.

One of my clients increased their OKR Leadership scores from 23% to 68% in 6 months. They now use OKR Leadership to drive most of their business decisions.

How about you? To what extent are you using OKR Leadership to drive your business?

3. Practice sharing your OKRs

OKR Leadership is not a private activity. Rather, OKR Leadership is a public management approach designed to solicit feedback, model accountability, and achieve outcomes. That's the reason why, when I lead OKR Leadership workshops, participants practice sharing their OKRs repeatedly — in conversation, in writing, and on video. Then I recommend that they share their OKRs with 10+ stakeholders within the next 24 hours.

Take a minute to write OKRs for your career, team, or organization.

Pause here.

Writing OKRs is not hard for most people, but like anything new, it can be hard to get started. You can go back and review the TIPS summary in Chapter 2 if you are having any difficulty. You can use the formula below in Figure 4.1.

However, implementing OKR Leadership is challenging.

Figure 4.1: Writing three elements

Three Elements of OKRs

1. **Verb:** Improve Customer Retention
2. **Outcome:** By 15%
3. **Deadline:** By the end of Q419

The OKR Formula: *"From X to Y by date"*

When I lead workshops, I invite people to write 3-4 Objectives. Then I invite people to select **only one** big objective to focus on. The most successful people, featured in every business book throughout history, have one objective. When you keep your obsessive focus on one big objective, then you will be more successful.

As an example, review the short video at www.action-learning.com > about to see how I make this point with audiences. This three-minute video is from a keynote address that I gave in March, 2019 to over 700 people. The main point of the video is that anyone can understand and practice OKR Leadership in any-sized team or organization.

4. Practice alignment

Getting a team perfectly aligned is a rare event. Most leaders take opportunities to state their mission and vision at times; but you also want to make certain that your OKRs support your organization's mission, vision and strategy.

Far too often, confusion about definitions can prevent team alignment from occurring. Imagine three different organizations, with three different approaches to alignment, as described in the next figure.

Figure 4.2. Mission, Vision and OKRs

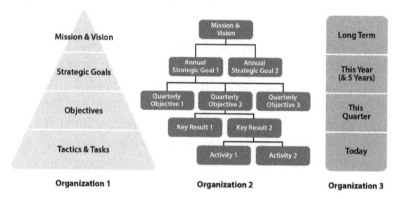

You may not know the mission, vision or strategy at your organization because it is changing in response to market demands or inconsistent leadership. That is normal.

I once had a client at a $50M retail business state that his OKRs focused on managing his business as a separate unit from the company. I coached him to adopt the vision of the organization if he wanted to remain an employee.

When people are confused about the mission, strategy or vision, they often create their own OKRs. Or they focus on activities and tasks to explain "how busy they are." People always create order out of chaos. Instead of leaving them to create their own notions about how to drive their business, OKRs can serve as a bridge between your mission and your tasks.

Does your team or organization look more like organization 1, 2, or 3 in the figure above? Or does your organization look like something else?

5. Practice an accountability cadence.

I strongly recommend that you review your OKRs at least quarterly.

Employee engagement scores are a lagging indicator (not a leading indicator) of *HOW* you are providing feedback to others.

Study the OKR life cycle image in Figure 4.3 carefully. Then adopt a regular feedback cadence into your ongoing performance review schedule. Some technology companies favor a quarterly cadence because they are familiar with agile sprints that adopt that frequency. Some review OKRs monthly. I have a manufacturing client who has adopted an OKR review cadence every 60 days. The senior leader said, "My boss wants us to review our OKRs every two months, 6 times each year. So, I scheduled our OKR review sessions every 60 days, about one week before we meet with my boss, so that we have accurate data."

Figure 4.3: OKR life cycle cadence

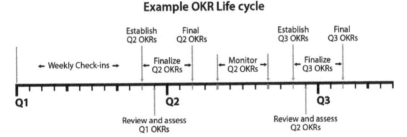

Clearly, one benefit of OKR Leadership is that this approach provides a regular cadence for managers and teams to review what they think are key objectives and results. OKR Leadership is a feedback process that *all* – not some — colleagues require and which *all* team members must participate.

6. Practice the AD-FIT™ coaching process

AD-FIT™ is the secret sauce of OKR Leadership – and it's something you can practice daily.

While managers are tasked with maximizing others' productivity, they're rarely taught how to do so. The AD-FIT™ coaching process is a protocol that managers use to do just that, and to determine whether their efforts are working.

Leaders also need to influence others' behaviors, but they too are rarely taught how to do so. The AD-FIT™ coaching process helps leaders do this and collectively build a better future.

What is coaching?

The answer to that question has defined my life and career to date. In 1997, I was developing leadership content with two business partners from Georgetown University and Johns Hopkins. My mentors declared, "Doug, you're a coach."

I replied, "Thank you. What's a coach?"

After decades of practicing coaching with hundreds of clients, multiple certifications, years of applied research, and my globally validated research on leader development, I can simplify the answer to my own question so many years ago by providing two definitions.

Academic definition: Coaching is a collaborative relationship or process designed for coachees practicing OKR Leadership to attain meaningful performance or business objectives (adapted from Green & Spence, 2014).

Practical definition: Coaching is the primary skill managers practice to maximize others' productivity.

Managers *need* to coach their direct reports for many good reasons. For one thing, internal coaching from managers is cost effective, shares organizational values, aligns activity with shared objectives, fosters teamwork and can reduce waste. There are protocols in finance, law, medicine and every mature profession that are designed to reduce risk and maximize outcomes. You can adopt these AD-FIT™ coaching protocols into your team or organization immediately.

External coaching is critical for senior leaders who require expertise and objectivity. Sadly, the practice of external coaching lacks protocols such as AD-FIT™. The result is market confusion and distrust.

As a disclosure, since 2013, I have been an executive coach and engagement manager with CoachSource, www.CoachSource.com, the world's largest provider of executive coaching, with over 1,200 expert executive coaches in 60+ countries. I have also served as an engagement manager with 5 global F500 companies that have demanded outcomes from expert executive coaches. I strongly recommend CoachSource for global breadth, deep expertise and integrity.

Why develop AD-FIT™ coaching protocols?

I developed and trademarked the AD-FIT coaching process in 2016 when three events collided.

At this time, I had a growing awareness of market confusion. Ever since 1997, when I started my company, I have met countless self-declared "professional consultants or coaches." Some are ethical, and well intentioned. Some, however, are not focused on client outcomes. The result is chaos in a marketplace crowded with skeptical buyers and inexperienced providers. Then, in 2016, three people asked the same question on the same day. Each person was a buying agent from a Fortune 500 organization – and each person wanted to know, "What is the actual ROI of any coaching investment?" They needed milestones and measures, based on a validated theoretical construct. They needed outcome-based protocols to sell the consulting investment to their managers and colleagues. I realized that the available survey data was not adequate for those buying agents to champion or sell organizational consulting services. Organizational clients needed outcome-based coaching protocols.

The second event occurred at the same time. A Fortune 500 healthcare client said, "We use protocols to mitigate risk and drive quality measures in healthcare. You have not described your coaching protocols. What are your they?" I stuttered, then gathered some milestones and best practices and labelled them "coaching protocols." I knew that protocols in healthcare can save lives or reduce waste. Protocols in consulting may contribute to leader outcomes, even though the consequences of *not* applying them wouldn't come with such dire results. Still, I knew that the term "protocol" carried weight. I trademarked the AD-FIT process in 2017 because my clients demanded a validated process. I adopted the word "protocols" because I realized that this term would likely contribute to the professionalism of consulting and coaching. In short, I felt that the coaching profession needed protocols.

The third event was the tipping point. After coaching hundreds of leaders in multiple sectors, I kept getting the same question: "What *really* works?" Individual leaders wanted an outcome-based process to achieve objectives and key results with efficiency. They wanted assessments, a list of outcomes, and evidence-based interventions that would accelerate leader development or provide them with a competitive advantage. The need for research to explore the potential relationship of coaching protocols on leader outcomes became even more clear. Individual leaders needed protocols.

When those three events collided, I began the formal research that eventually led to a globally validated coaching protocol. That is the short history for developing the AD-FIT™ coaching process.

All details on the AD-FIT™ coaching process, including some free digital courses, are described at www.action-learning.com or www.ADFIT.org **or www.OKR leadership.com.** My theoretical construct and business model is based on positive psychology. Research in organizational leadership clearly indicates that leaders flourish when you focus on the art and science of well-being. Consequently, the AD-FIT™ coaching protocols incorporate that research.

At a recent conference, when I presented the AD-FIT™ coaching process, a participant summarized it well. He said, "AD-FIT™ coaching process is both deep and wide, like the Mississippi River. It has to be deep enough to provide a simple structure for managers to implement. And it has to be wide enough to include any other content from any corner of the organization."

The AD-FIT™ coaching process has five steps:

1. A = **Assess** your individual strengths, weaknesses, blind spots and hidden talents
2. D = **Define** your meaningful outcomes / objectives / OKRs
3. F = **Focus** on your critical needs
4. I = **Implement** evidence-based interventions / interactions

5. T= **Take away** action steps that reward your desired outcomes / objectives

I encourage you to edit the form in Figure 4.4 below for your career, team or organization. I recommend a one-page form with rows to track behavior and performance changes over time. The heading includes the name of the direct report, the date of the coaching meeting, and the primary outcomes that were discussed. For instance, if the primary outcome is business development, then the comments in each row include any of their notes about action steps or required resources for business development. See the example below for a coaching session that Jill conducted with her direct report named Michael.

Figure 4.4: Sample AD-FIT™ Coaching Form

Coaching Form for XYZ Organization				Date:
Manager's Name: Jill Williams	Title:			
Direct Report's Name: Michael Jones	Title:			
Primary Outcome: *Increase business development* 3% y/year by Q2				
Action 1:	Resources required:	Measures by date 1:	Measures by date 2:	How completion demonstrated:
Call all level 1 prospects by month 2	Call list, sales script, target client notes	60 calls/day, 100% client notes updated	...plus 5 prospect meetings/ week by month 2	Weekly activity summaries sent to Jill, monthly new business summaries posted to team
Action 2:				

Let's walk through a more detailed explanation for practicing AD-FIT™ coaching in your OKR Leadership.

AD = The A and D aspects of the AD-FIT™ process describe what you are doing with each direct report, client or colleague over time. I strongly recommend that you keep a digital folder to track each person's OKRs. The template in Figure 11 can be edited for any organization, or for self-coaching.

A = Assess the strengths and mindset of others. We all have strengths and weaknesses. We all have blind spots (self-ratings are lower than other-ratings) and we all have hidden talents (self-ratings are lower than other-ratings.) People flourish when they focus on their signature strengths, and languish when they focus on their weaknesses or deficits.

Mindsets determine the probability of effective AD-FIT™ coaching. You'll recall our discussion about fixed vs. growth mindsets. Well, people with fixed mindsets cannot be coached or managed. People with growth mindsets can be coached and managed — because they will learn how to implement OKRs. A simple assessment of mindset is the question, "To what extent are you willing to change?" (0-60% is a fixed mindset, over 61% is a growth mindset)

I favor using any validated assessments that is endorsed by you or your client's organization. There are over 15,000 validated assessments. I do not use unreliable or invalid "assessments" such as Myers-Briggs or anything that purports to minimize the complexity of human behavior into 9 boxes, 3 colors or 4 animals. Be wary of such silly distractions. If you need free validated assessments of individual or team strengths, then I recommend https://www.viacharacter.org/ or https://www.authentichappiness.sas.upenn.edu/home questionnaires.

I typically use a valid and reliable personality survey such as the Hogan suite, a behavioral assessment such as DISC, an Emotional Intelligence survey, and a values survey such as the Personal Inventories Attitudes and Values assessment with my individual clients. I also use qualitative stakeholder interviews and quantitative data assessments of business measures with my organizational clients.

D = define a meaningful outcome or objective for your OKRs. No surprise here: outcome-based coaching requires that you define a meaningful objective. Then you must adopt milestones to measure your progress.

There are two types of outcomes. In one of my global research studies, the top two *performance* outcomes *(n* =100 responses) were increased productivity and focus. The top two *behavior* outcomes (*n* =115 responses) were improved relationships and effectiveness. When I provide outcome-based coaching and consulting solutions, I always offer a list of 30-40 possible outcomes. Clients then select their top three choices. Often, those three outcomes are the three objectives selected for their OKRs. I recommend using the terms Outcomes = Objectives interchangeably when applying the AD-FIT™ process.

Review the lists in Figure 4.5 below until you define your top outcomes. Then post your outcomes in a visible location. Review them at the start of every coaching session — and reward desired behaviors when you attain milestones.

Your task: select up to three of the following outcomes, then determine how to measure each. You can add your own outcomes if useful.

Figure 4.5: Sample AD-FIT™ coaching outcomes

Top executive coaching outcomes:	Top business coaching outcomes:
o Business Acumen o Career Development o Change Management o Coaching & Developing Others o Communication Skills o Creativity / Innovation o Critical Thinking o Customer Focus o Diversity and Inclusion o Emotional Intelligence o Empowering Others / Delegation o Executive Presence o Global Mindset / Intercultural Effectiveness o Influencing Others o Integrity o Managing Up o Performance Management o Political Savvy o Presentation Skills / Public Speaking o Relationships & Networking o Self-Development / Self-Insight o Teambuilding o Time Management/ Work-Life Balance o Transition Management / "First 90 Days" o Treating People with Respect o Vision and Strategy	o Banking and financing o Board of directors/advisors o Branding o Change management o Communication skills o Compensation and benefits o Computer security o Conflict resolution o Customer service o Ethics o Insurance / risk management o Leadership assessments o Managing growth o Managing others o Marketing o Operations o Personal finances o Personal health and well-being o Presentation skills o Safety/ workers compensation o Sales o Talent development o Time/energy management

○ [Please add your own] ○	○ [Please add your own] ○

Many people struggle to quantify milestones. They often need a manager or accountability coach to help them implement OKR Leadership. I typically use action plan templates to quantify milestones in outcome-based coaching engagements, and then adapt those templates for each of my individual and organizational clients.

So, to recap: I use the "A and D steps" to describe each coaching engagement. I then use the "FIT steps" – which describe what you are doing with each direct report or colleague — in each coaching session or discussion. The AD-FIT™ coaching process is instrumental when tracking the feedback process using OKRs. It can be applied to developing outcome-based relationships with any clients, direct reports, colleagues or loved ones. Let's look at the "FIT Steps" in more detail.

F = Focus on your outcomes. I encourage you to start each session by asking, "What do you want to focus on today?" Both you and your direct report (or client) should take notes to model engaged learning. The opening focus may change during your session to a deeper, more meaningful focus. When using OKRs the KR structure helps both of you to focus on what is measurable and what resources may be required. The focus of your session may be predefined based on your direct report's outcomes, or it may change in response to your direct report's (or client's) new business needs.

I = Interventions or interactions or best practices. When we have problems we require and often seek solutions from managers and consultants. As we have discussed, interactions with others provide feedback, and feedback leads to learning. Psychologists describe interventions as "what really works." You may find it helpful to use the OKR worksheet in chapter 2 to structure each AD-FIT™ coaching session.

I typically provide some evidence-based content and structure for each coaching session. For instance, if one of my client's outcomes is to develop executive presence, then I will provide a slide presentation, or best practices for review. Those proprietary documents are tremendously valuable. I encourage my clients to save them in a digital folder called "Action Learning Associates" or "Executive Coaching."

I favor evidence-based practices because there is so much silly content now available online. Be wary. It can be hard to separate what is valuable from what is not, given the abundance of choices. For examples, digital courses, and videos of evidence-based solutions I recommend that you visit www.action-learning.com or www.ADFIT.org or www.OKRleadership.com.

T = Takeaways or next steps. The purpose of this final step is to model accountability and desired changes. I will typically ask, "What are you taking away from this session today that you intend to do before our next session?" I encourage both you and your direct report to take notes and record your responses. I strongly encourage you to review the action plan matrix monthly. Then take more notes. If your direct report does not take notes, or does not take action, then you are tolerating poor performance. Managers do not do – and should not – do anyone else's OKR work. Each person must practice their own OKR Leadership, because they are managing their own business.

Finally, I often ask, "How compliant have you been with the AD-FIT™ coaching protocols since our last session?" I consider low compliance low compliance to be 0-20%, 20-40%, 60-80%; high compliance is 80-100%? You can see that this sets the bar high for compliance. While there are no right / wrong answers, coaching is more successful when leaders are at least 80% compliant with the AD-FIT™ coaching protocols.

When I ask "To what extent are you using OKR Leadership to drive your business?" I often get scores of 20-40%. But when I ask, "To what extent SHOULD you use OKR Leadership to drive your business?" I often get scores of 80-100%.

How about your career? Your team? Your organization?

I know the AD-FIT™ process works. I have globally validated it through research, and practiced it since 1997 with thousands of leaders. Try it. Odds are, you'll find the same results if you try it and begin applying it using the contents of this chapter as a workbook for review every quarter.

Key points from Chapter 4, How do you practice OKR Leadership?

1. Coaching is the primary skill managers practice to maximize others' productivity.

2. Managers and leaders can use the globally validated AD-FIT™ coaching process to provide feedback. The AD-FIT™ process is an evidence-based approach to positive psychology coaching or consulting based upon (a) awareness of strengths and growth mindset, (b) defining a meaningful objective or OKRs, (c) focus on the client's agenda, (d) interventions and interaction, (e) takeaways, and (f) percentage of compliance to this model. Trademarked and globally validated by Action Learning Associates, LLC, 2018.

3. You need to practice asking great questions, especially those that begin with "what" and "how." I use the OKR Pulse Survey question to measure adoption and organizational change over time. That question is, "To what extent are you using OKR Leadership to drive your business?" Score from 1 (low) to 10 (high).

4. You need to practice writing and sharing your OKRs. This is a public management approach designed to solicit feedback, model accountability and achieve outcomes.

5. You can make certain that your OKRs align with the mission, vision and strategy of your team or organization. People always create "order" out of chaos.

6. I recommend that you review your OKRs quarterly. OKRs are a feedback process that ALL colleagues require.

Key questions from chapter 4, How do you practice OKR Leadership?

1. Use the OKR Pulse Survey Question regularly. Ask your direct reports and clients, "To what extent do you use OKR Leadership to drive your business?" Score from 1 (low) to 10 (high) like the Net Promoter Score.
2. What evidence can you provide to demonstrate that you are practicing a growth mindset?
3. How do you know if you are asking great questions? What unsolicited feedback do you receive from your direct reports or clients?
4. Have you shared your OKRs with 10+ stakeholders in your career, team or organization?
5. How are you practicing alignment with your organization's mission, vision and strategy?
6. What is your OKR Leadership accountability cadence?
7. What is your system for practicing AD-FIT™ coaching with your direct reports or clients?

Chapter 5. OKR Leadership and Career Development

Fictional dialog

Karl: Only 20-somethings talk about career development. As if *anything* is possible.

John: Are you kidding? Everyone I know is looking on LinkedIn or Zip Recruiter for their next position. I bookmark Glassdoor so that I can check out new opportunities every day.

Alice: That may explain why so many surveys describe low engagement scores. 30% across industries. Unchanged for decades. And low productivity at my organization. Dilbert comics are my reality.

John: You aren't alone. It seems like everyone is perpetually in career transition. People aspire for the next better opportunity. People are resilient. We adapt and overcome. We always look for the next best whatever... job, career, apartment, life partner... And we tolerate those mediocre people in our organizations because we think they may leave someday soon.

Enrique: Yikes. What a dark view of career development.

Question: Which of these characters reflects what you are currently thinking about OKR Leadership?

Key points

1. Work can be described over your lifespan as either a job, a career or a calling.
2. Some people are perpetually in career transition.

3. OKR Leadership can be a career development process in your 20s, 30s, 40s, 50s — truly, at any age.
4. The primary objective of this chapter is to help any reader apply the OKR Leadership process to your personal career development – and to recognize that OKR Leadership matters for your career.
5. A secondary objective of this chapter is to help any practitioner accelerate the career development of others using OKR Leadership. Leadership matters for others on your team.

Definitions

We've already defined, leadership: the ability to influence behavior toward a better future. I've also shared one of the main assumptions in this book — that humans are aspirational. My experience is that all humans desire to create a better future for themselves and for their loved ones. Ask anyone holding a newborn child, or on commencement day, or after accepting a job promotion.

Yet too often, we hear people talk about career development with a sense of confusion. They lack clarity about definitions. So, I've decided to open this chapter with three definitions based on new research on positive psychology.

When you explore career development you need to start by asking, "How do you describe your reason for work?" Specifically, is your reason for working a job, a career or a calling?

These three definitions are critical for a discussion of career development. A job is defined as the activity that provides money and sustenance. A career is a series of jobs that provide opportunity, meaning or purpose. A calling is comprised of significant activities that provide meaning or serve a purpose larger than oneself.

To be clear: there is nothing wrong or right about using any one of these three definitions to describe your reason for working. Your answer will simply help you to determine where to go from here.

> Is your reason for working a job,
> a career or a calling?

Let's start this chapter with a short research question.

If you were to ask one thousand physicians how they would describe their work, how do you think they would answer?

a) Most would describe their work as a calling because they are providing critical health care for others
b) Most would describe their work as a career because they are required to demonstrate competence in a series of demanding roles with increased regulation from healthcare administrators, insurers, and consumer-generated social media
c) Most would describe their work as a job because they have over $250,000 in college tuition debt and higher burnout than any other professionals

Now pause for a moment to reflect on your answer.

Whatever bucket you selected most likely reflects *your* answer to the question, "How would you describe your reason for working?"

The answer to the question using a sample population of physicians is that roughly one-third of survey respondents who are physicians respond in each of those three buckets.[1] Are you surprised by that finding?

Now let's change the sample population for the same research question. If you were to ask one thousand janitors how they would describe their work, how do you think they would answer?

a) Most would describe their work as a calling because they are providing critical cleaning services that enable others to excel
b) Most would describe their work as a career because they are trusted to clean facilities without much supervision
c) Most would describe their work as a job because they have an endless need to do repetitious work with low levels of compensation

The answer for janitors is that, once again, roughly one-third of survey respondents fall in each of those three buckets. That research question has been replicated in other sample populations, including retail sales, public service and healthcare.[2]

If you are surprised by these findings, then perhaps you should look in the mirror.

Let's extrapolate a bit and assume that one-third of the candidates for every position represent each of these three buckets. If you are in transition, then roughly one-third of the roles you are considering will be a more likely organization fit. The remaining two-thirds of the roles can be removed from your list because they are not consistent with your work bucket. If you are developing a talent pipeline or career ladder within your organization, know that roughly one-third of your current and future employees are represented by each of these three buckets.

Let's assume that you self-reflect enough to know which bucket you are in. Again — there is nothing wrong or right about being in any of them. However, if you want to change your mind set about work, then you need to adopt this approach: "My mindset is that work is a ___." "Work can be more meaningful for me if I adopt ___."

Practicing OKR Leadership requires aspiration and direction, the will and the way.

If you are in career transition, then you probably struggle to answer the question, "what do you do?" Work defines most people. And while we spend many hours "at work," we don't often talk about the psychology of work. In post-industrial cultures like the U.S., you may regard work as both an economic necessity for survival, and a meaningful pursuit. Working is certainly necessary for material rewards. You need to pay the rent or mortgage. You need to feed yourself and your loved ones. Working may also provide meaningful ways for you to measure achievement, social connection, or power. The centrality of work in our lives cannot be ignored.[3]

How you regard your career makes a difference if you are considering applying OKR Leadership to your career. Developmental psychologists today often use the lifespan model in Figure 5.1 below, from Donald Super, to describe the influence of three variables at any stage in life.[4] Consider your role and the impact of environmental factors (e.g., labor market, local economies, global economies), situational factors (e.g., social, economic, racial, historical) and personal factors (e.g. psychological traits, behavioral patterns, intelligence) to describe the choices available to you at any season of your career. Where are you located on this career lifespan model?

Figure 5.1: Career lifespan model

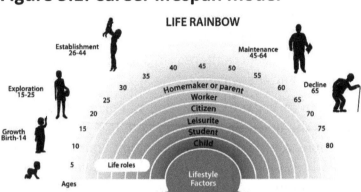

(Concept used with permission from Donald Super.)

Career Development Questions

When I provide career coaching and consulting I often make the point that career objectives change depending upon the decade in your career lifecycle. On average, college graduates in the U.S. today will have 5-7 careers and over 12 different job titles. Many of those job titles have not been developed yet, and many combine traits and expertise, such as consultant/ cyber teacher/ author or sales expert/ healthcare advocate/ lobbyist. If you are curious about career trends, then I recommend searching resources from Pew Research Center, the Kauffman Foundation, Forrester Research and all professional associations related to your career.

There are countless digital resources for career development questions. Any search phrase such as "behavioral interview top questions" or "resume editing" will lead to dozens of targeted advertisements from vendors hawking their services. Annual survey data from publications such as *Inc., Entrepreneur, Forbes, The Wall Street Journal* or *The New York Times* may be useful. Annual career development surveys from universities and colleges may be useful. Of course, those survey results and questions are never sufficient – because your career development is unique.

When I provide career development coaching I use the following questions to prompt discussion. I then encourage clients to write their objectives and key results, as described in the 4 examples below. If you are in a career transition, then I recommend that you write your answers to the following questions – then share them with your accountability partners or career consultant. Ask for feedback. I have used these questions with students at Vanderbilt University's Owen School of Business for several years.

1. What do you want to focus on in your next career phase?
2. How accurate is your resume?
3. What is your elevator pitch, or your career brand or unique selling proposition (USP)?
4. What values are important to you, and why? How will those values influence your career choices?
5. What professional and personal mentors have influenced you, and why? How do you plan to leverage 5-6 professional mentors in the future?
6. What are your career development goals at each decade in your career lifespan?
7. What is your typical role at work? How are you stretching or experimenting when working with others? What could you change in your next career?
8. Assessments often lead to learning. Based on your career assessments, what are your strengths, weaknesses, blind spots and hidden strengths?

9. How are you building your career narratives about yourself (e.g., answers to common interview questions, preparation for behavioral interviews)? Have you written down and video recorded your career narratives? Do you have a professional digital twin with photos and videos that convey your expertise? Have you practiced describing your career narratives with 3-5 people who will provide critical feedback?

Career Development Tips

The following short list of tips that have worked well for many of my clients going through career transition. I strongly recommend that you organize your transition with spreadsheets and daily activity logs. Create a career transition spreadsheet with your key 3-5 variables (e.g., job role, organizational reputation, location, initial compensation, role potential, compensation or skill potential, key values, etc.) Write your primary objective and two to five KRs for that objective. Then write your secondary objective and key results. Share your KRs with 4-5 accountability partners in a weekly cadence. If you need a career transition scoresheet see Figure 5.2 below. Note that each activity has a number of points attached to it. We all need to measure what matters. This template has helped dozens of my clients.

Figure 5.2: Career Transition Scoresheet

Name: _____

Scoring for the week of _____ to _____

	Sun.	Mon.	Tue.	Wed.	Thu.	Fri.	Sat.
Face to face interview 10 pts.							
Face to face meeting 5 pts.							
Ask for referral 5 pts.							
Phone call 2 pts.							
Email 1 pt.							
Total points for the day							
Cumulative point total for week							

Scoring for the week of _____ to _____

	Sun.	Mon.	Tue.	Wed.	Thu.	Fri.	Sat.
Face to face interview 10 pts.							
Face to face meeting 5 pts.							
Ask for referral 5 pts.							
Phone call 2 pts.							
Email 1 pt.							
Total points for the day							
Cumulative point total for week							

Scoring for the week of _____ to _____

	Sun.	Mon.	Tue.	Wed.	Thu.	Fri.	Sat.
Face to face interview 10 pts.							
Face to face meeting 5 pts.							
Ask for referral 5 pts.							
Phone call 2 pts.							
Email 1 pt.							
Total points for the day							
Cumulative point total for week							

Scoring for the week of _____ to _____

	Sun.	Mon.	Tue.	Wed.	Thu.	Fri.	Sat.
Face to face interview 10 pts.							
Face to face meeting 5 pts.							
Ask for referral 5 pts.							
Phone call 2 pts.							
Email 1 pt.							
Total points for the day							
Cumulative point total for week							

When you consider working at organization X or Y, determine your organizational fit (e.g., job, career, calling). Use the template in Figure 5.3 below to create a scoresheet for your career development, and then create a KR to rate your organizational fit (you can score from 1-10, or use a red-yellow-green formula). Your variables for organizational fit could include location, leadership team, future compensation, predicted market changes, reputational, leadership trust index (LTI), etc. I encourage you to edit the worksheet below to include your key variables.

Figure 5.3: Organizational Fit Scoresheet

Organization name	location	Leadership team (1-10)	Future compensation (1-10)	Market changes (1-10)	LTI (1-10)	Score (1-10)
Company x	10 mins	4	3	6	4	17
Company y	30 mins	7	7	3	8	25

Based on this example, company x is located closer, so the commute would be shorter. But the leadership team and leadership trust index (LTI) is low. The future compensation is also low and the market threats are high. Therefore, if this leader can overcome the location challenge, Company y may be a better organizational fit at this point in time.

Career Development Quiz

There is a great deal of confusion in the world of career development. If yo9u are in a career transition, then I encourage you to take this short quiz about technology, integrity, resumes and referrals. Are the following statements true or false?

1. Talent selection software algorithms review online applications and digitally discard over 90% of applications. True or false?
2. About 30% of resumes contain inaccurate information. True or false?

3. Interviewers spend less than 6 seconds reading resumes. True or false?
4. Most career transitions succeed as a result of direct referrals. True or false?

Write down your answers.

FYI, the answer to each of these statements is true. If you are surprised to learn that, then your blind spots may include technology, integrity, interviews or referrals.

Technology organizes data. In particular, resume-assessment and hiring software is designed to sort applicants based on matching key words, job requirements, potential fit, and how quickly you provide contact information for recommendations. Vendor companies such as Zip Recruiter, Monster, and Cornerstone partner with recruiting companies such as Vaco and Randstad to digitally discard the majority of applicants. The CHRO at Amazon recently stated that their 40% annual growth rate requires that they automate hiring and selection. Many jobs that require data organization and assessment will be robotized. However, jobs that require curiosity and empathy will always require creative people with critical minds. A very simplified view of the future is that there will be two kinds of careers: those in which robots will supervise humans (e.g., manufacturing, insurance claims, banking) and those in which humans will supervise robots (e.g., data analysts, health care assistants, sales consultants).[5]

Integrity is critical. Multiple studies confirm that resumes continue to be inaccurate, even though applicants are encouraged to check details that can be validated in online databases such as LinkedIn.[6] If you state that you have related experience, then get hired and cannot demonstrate your ability to do that work, then your low integrity will shorten your employment. Integrity will always be critical in your career.

Interviews are subjective and inefficient. Most recruiters are over worked and compensated based on the number of interviews conducted, or candidates hired, not by the organizational fit or retention after 24 months. Digital interviews are less expensive than direct interviews, and vendors such as HireVue claim that they are more accurate.

And perhaps most importantly: referrals matter. Reputations lead to referrals, and probably always will be the most relevant predictor of career transitions.

Career development examples

To emphasize the fact that career development can take place at any point in your life, the following four examples of OKR Leadership come from leaders in their 20s, 30s, 40s and 50s. Regardless of your age, you can learn from each example.

OKR Leadership in your 20s

Let's look first at a recent college graduate. Amy majored in pre-medicine because her family members had encouraged her to become a physician. She studied for the MCAT examinations and earned strong test scores. However, she also developed anxiety attacks that required medication. She became a medical scribe and spent 12 months working at one of the premier hospitals in the country. After a year of working, Amy wanted to assess whether healthcare was her career or her calling.

I helped Amy get an idea of her strengths, weaknesses, blind spots and hidden talents. She took several assessments include the Big Five personality assessment, and a vocational aptitude assessment. After 6 months, she determined that her new objective was to leverage her clinical care experience into a medical sales career. Her initial KRs included developing her resume and cover letter, recommendations and digital profile. Her next KRs included soliciting advice from 3-5 healthcare leaders each week, taking detailed notes on a spreadsheet, and asking each, "What do you think would be a good fit for me, and who do you recommend that I meet?"

Once Amy clarified her new OKRs into weekly actions, she was able to solicit feedback and develop her reputation. The chief physician she worked with went to the hospital administrator and said, "We are going to lose her unless you hire her into your department immediately." The administrator offered her a position within days.

Then one of the most senior nurses sent a text to her brother, a sales manager at a nearby F500 healthcare company. The brother called Amy back immediately. He said, "In over 20 years, my sister has never recommended anyone because she is so demanding. I trust her referral implicitly. Send me your contact information today. Let me recommend you to our inside sales account executive. We need people like you immediately."

OKR Leadership is a decision-making framework that enabled this recent college graduate to transition into a role that helped her assess whether healthcare was her calling. Amy re-designed her OKRs around a new career objective in medical sales. Then she used the KRs to define critical actions in her digital and direct applications. But the most important KR for her, and for you, was to ask for feedback based on her reputation.

TIPS for career development in your 20s:

1. Build your career development team.
2. Develop your resume and LinkedIn profile.
3. Manage your digital twin and digital reputation by un-tagging and un-friending any questionable digital content or contacts.
4. Ask 3-5 leaders each week for feedback and referrals.
5. Take detailed notes in your spreadsheet.
6. Ask, "What do you think would be a good fit for me, and who do you recommend that I should meet?"
7. Assume that you will have many career options.

OKR Leadership in your 30s

Now let's look at a newly-promoted manager in his 30s. Tom was often "the life of the party" and appreciated for his capacity to find humor in almost any situation. His extroversion, good looks and quick laugh enabled him to excel in sales. His manager said, "We expanded territories. We increased goals over 20% annually. We changed product lines – and Tom always remained in the top 5% of sales. So, we promoted him to a sales manager."

Top producers are often promoted into manager roles. But newly-promoted managers are rarely ready. They always require internal coaching and training on protocols for maximizing others' performance, and don't often receive validated protocols such as OKR Leadership or the AD-FIT™ coaching process.

Tom represents many newly-promoted managers who need to learn how to coach others. He was the primary revenue provider in his family, with a schedule that demanded overnight travel 3-4 days each week. His wife worked part time from home They had two young children. In our first session together, Tom said, "Typically I win every challenge in front of me. But I don't know how to manage the demands of work and home. I'm terrified that I will fail."

I was contracted to be Tom's executive coach because he needed to manage his work, life and career. Like many readers of this book, his primary objective was to meet the requirements of his new role and support his family.

His first KR was to provide weekly status updates for his manager on the OKRs of his direct reports. Tom wanted to manage up because scorecards were familiar, and his manager demanded weekly status updates. KR2 was to conduct bi-weekly one-on-one sessions with his seven direct reports. Tom adopted the 10-10-10 structure for each 30-minute meeting. In the first 10 minutes Tom shared his objectives and agenda. In the second 10 minutes, his direct report did the same. Then, in the last 10 minutes they determined next steps and resource requirements. Perhaps like many readers of this book, KR3 was to express his love for his wife and children with daily behaviors. Tom spent at least 30 minutes daily playing with each of his children. Tom practiced validating his wife without expectations daily. When traveling, Tom always used Skype or FaceTime for 10-15 minutes in the morning and another 10-15 minutes in the evening to connect with his family members. KR4 was to practice coaching others using the AD-FIT™ coaching process.

TIPS for career development in your 30s:

1. Practice all the tips listed above.
2. Career development requires learning new skills. Adopt a growth mindset (e.g., "I can try this") instead of a fixed mindset (e.g., "that will never work") when confronted with new demands.

3. Ask questions that begin with "What" and "How" to explore multiple solutions with others.
4. Adopt the perspective that "good enough" is better than "perfection" when pursuing your OKRs.
5. Thank those on your career development team weekly. Gratitude can open doors of possibility.

OKR Leadership in your 40s

Now let's look at an operations manager in her 40s. Lori worked as a contractor for several years when her children were in grade school. Then she was hired into a sales role, then an account manager role, and then promoted to an operations manager in her 40s. She exceeded expectations in her annual performance reviews, and struggled to raise her children as a single parent. Lori worked from home in the evenings and weekends to "keep up with email demands." Others described her as "demanding, detailed, just impossible to keep up with."

I worked as Lori's executive coach to assess her strengths and weaknesses, provide more objective feedback, and recommend performance or behavior outcomes to accelerate her career. In our first meeting, Lori said, "I'm not here because I want to be. My manager said that I need to work with an executive coach to modify my behaviors. But I'm not sure what that means."

No one wants to be fixed. People typically resist changing their behavior for two reasons: either they do not know *what* to change, or they do not accept *why* they need to change. Lori represented both.

In our initial sessions, Lori developed trust with me and shared her perspective on the organization. As part of her assessment, I spoke to 6-8 of her colleagues to assess their perspective on her strengths, weakness and future.

If two or more people stated a similar point, I collected that feedback into categorical themes. I took the results from these conversations and wrote a confidential summary for Lori.

Lori told me that she was "shattered by the feedback" and required 24 hours to reflect. Then she "took it to heart."

Lori's new objective was to be a more effective leader. She understood that she was a zealous manager who maximized others' productivity by modelling excellence and efficiency. She was too demanding, did not provide enough positive feedback, and shared her criticism without offering solutions. In short, Lori was not influencing her direct reports toward a better vision of the future.

KR1 was to model optimism by making more positive statements than negative statements in all internal meetings. Lori used a tally sheet with two columns in her notebook. We discussed her positive and negative interactions tally sheet weekly. KR2 was to provide two to three solutions for every critical judgement in all internal meetings. Lori literally wrote *scripts* prior to strategy meetings using a complete communication wheel to separate data, emotions, judgements, wants and wills. KR3 was to request a champion in the room to provide behavioral feedback at any time if Lori was too forceful or not providing solutions. Those text messages (e.g., make sure you listen to Fred) quickly modified Lori's behavior, and reinforced her trust in that champion.

It took only a few months for Lori's colleagues to recognize her as a more positive leader. Then, she was offered a promotion. When speaking at trade conferences, she was often approached by recruiters and leaders from other organizations. Those external validations were kind, but Lori's words were better; "For the first time in my career, I knew that I had choices. I could stay. I could leave. I could provide for my children. I did not need to re-marry or follow anyone else. I stepped into my own shoes as a leader."

TIPS for career development in your 40s:

1. Practice all the tips listed above.
2. Build your career development team.
3. Practice new behaviors using internal champions and external feedback. Regularly solicit feedback from others.
4. Practice new behaviors in a mirror or record your objectives using a smart phone.
5. Seek to understand the feedback, then reflect, then adopt a different perspective.
6. Practice optimism instead of pessimism, especially in public.
7. Practice leadership by serving as a board member for any related professional organization.

OKR Leadership in your 50s

Finally, we'll look at a 53 year-old senior leader in a Fortune 100 company. Jeff was hired from the banking and finance sector to work in manufacturing because of his capacity to integrate digital infrastructure security systems. He accepted the offer because the Chief Financial Officer (CFO) and Chief Executive Officer (CEO) described him as a "velocity hire." No one defined the term "velocity hire," but Jeff assumed that term meant that they would provide career development opportunities for broader operational responsibilities.

Within 3 years, he developed the digital infrastructure required to manage over 3,000 people and a $900M budget. As the CFO at a former employer, Jeff had managed over 5,000 people and a $1.5 trillion budget, including a sales operation P/L of over $1 trillion per year. He felt under-utilized in his new role and requested broader or deeper operational responsibilities. Within five years Jeff received several special projects, and was asked to serve as a board member for an internal new company. But he was not promoted. Along with about seven other peers, Jeff aspired to be the next CFO.

In a recent executive coaching session, Jeff stated, "I have just been told that Stan will be the next CFO, not me. Now I need to determine what is my next career development move."

I was hired by his employer to be his executive coach and help Jeff explore his career transition options.

Like many senior leaders, Jeff's family lived in a different city from where his office was located. That fact meant that Jeff traveled extensively and stayed in a corporate hotel five or six nights every week. His wife and adult children supported his career ambition. Everyone recognized his expertise and capacity to work as a C-suite leader (e.g., CFO, COO, CTO, CIO) in virtually any business sector.

Jeff's new objective was to define a clear future within 30 days. KR1 was to have a one on one meeting with Stan within the week to tell his data story and leave a copy of his resume so that Stan would know his capacity. Jeff had a current resume, but there was no reason for Stan to know Jeff's data story or expertise. KR2 was to have three meetings within 30 days with C-suite leaders from Fortune 500 companies in his home town. Jeff had a list of the companies, and had previously avoided such invitations to meet. KR3 was to have at least four confidential meetings with executive recruiters with a demonstrated history of successful retained search placements. Jeff had not responded to the eight or so queries per month that he had received over the past five years because he did not want to be distracted from his current job.

Like many readers of this book, Jeff explored all of these KRs within thirty days. He was promoted into a new role as a CIO.

TIPS for career development in your 50s:

1. Practice all the tips listed above.
2. Build your career development team of champions, mentors, and recruiters.
3. Develop your data story (e.g., facts about your career that others would not necessarily know) and create a lengthy referral list.
4. Make sure that your LinkedIn profile reflects your current value.
5. Make sure that your resume quantifies your achievements.
6. Assume that in today's competitive talent economy you will have unique value to another employer.
7. Deliberately associate yourself with the promotion agents inside your organization, as well as the hiring agents from multiple other organizations.
8. Assume that you will have many career options at each point in your career.

Key points from Chapter 5, OKR Leadership and Career Development"

1. OKR Leadership can be a career development process for you to practice what matters next, at any age.
2. A job is defined as the activity that provides you with money and sustenance.

3. A career is defined as a series of jobs that provide you with opportunity, meaning or purpose.
4. A calling is defined as meaningful activities that provide you with meaning or serve a purpose larger than yourself.
5. Career development requires practicing new skills with a new accountability team. Individuals do not win, teams win.

Key questions from Chapter 5, OKR Leadership and Career Development

1. Would you describe your attitude toward work today as a job, career or a calling?
2. How many careers have you had to date? If you were to have three to five more careers, how might you describe those careers? If you were to describe your next career with slashes (e.g., a consultant/writer/teacher or a programmer/CEO), then what could your next three to five careers possibly be?
3. What activity do you do that leads to a flow state (a balance of challenge and skills) that someone would pay you to do?
4. What activity do you do that leads others to state, "Thank you, that was valuable"?
5. How are you serving others today? Specifically, how do you know that you are providing value or quality to others? How many others do you serve each year? How many others do you want to serve next year?
6. How are you providing for your physical needs in the last 20 years of your life? What social support will be ideal? How much money will you need? Where would you like to live?

CHAPTER 6: FAMILY LEADERSHIP AND OKR LEADERSHIP

Fictional dialog

Alice: My parents always said there was a book. But I never got a copy.

Karl: Huh? What are you talking about?

Alice: That book that tells people how to be a better parent. *Parenting for Dummies*. Do you have that book?

John: I wish. That book doesn't exist. My experience is that most family members are confused about their roles.

Alice: I definitely have confusion. One minute I need to be a manager, as Super Mom, maximizing productivity. Then I quickly need to be a leader, influencing others' behavior. When our kids were young I complained about them all the time.

Karl: Yes, I remember. You were sleep deprived. Now your kids are in their 20s, and you're still confused.

John: One way I reduce confusion is to state my role, as Big Daddy, out loud. When I state, "As a leader in this family business, we need to listen to one another during our family meeting," others know my role – and they know my expectations for their behavior.

Enrique: Right. And at work I should state, "As a manager in this business we need to reduce expenses without losing our key employees."

John: Yes. The myth is that OKR Leadership only occurs during work hours. But this approach is critical for family business leaders because they represent about 70% of the U.S. economy. And about 70% of new job creation.

Karl: My uncle owns a small business. He says that all family business leaders worry about succession planning.

John: Yes. The failure to plan and manage succession is the greatest threat to family business succession. Succession planning and ownership problems are complex; in fact they represent a multi-trillion dollar problem in the U.S. Baby boomers do not know how to assess their business and recommend changes. Consultants do not know best practices that work. They need information and guidance on how to do so.

Question: Which of these characters reflects what you are currently thinking about OKR Leadership?

Key points in this chapter

1. **The primary objective** of this chapter is to define the problem of family leadership for family members, owners and consultants.
2. **A secondary objective** of this chapter is to provide examples of how you can apply OKR Leadership to a family-owned business
3. Family leaders (e.g., matriarchs, patriarchs, passive, remote, surrogate, unacceptable) try their best, but they lack leadership skills.
4. Family-owned business leaders require OKR Leadership to practice what matters next. Examples include succession planning, cost reduction and organizational change.

Problems

This chapter addresses two problems that exist in most cultures. The first problem is that many family leaders — e.g., matriarchs, patriarchs, passive, remote, surrogate, unacceptable — lack leadership skills. The second problem is that most family business leaders do not practice OKR Leadership; which means that they don't practice or measure what matters most. The result is that many family members are reactive when they need to be proactive.

Family leaders try their best

You may not agree, or have personally experienced, that most family leaders lack leadership skills. But there is abundant evidence for bad communication, divorce, domestic violence, and domestic conflict. And even if your experiences are not as dire as these, every family leader I've ever met has struggles.

While that fact is not new, our awareness and acknowledgement of those struggles *is* new. 4,500 years of recorded history provide countless examples of family leaders who lack leadership skills. Consider one cultural lens— religion. Christians cite examples from the Old Testament and Jesus, using characters such as Adam and Eve, Jacob and Esau, Cain and Abel. Muslims cite examples from the Prophet Mohammed and the Qur'an to the extended family of believers called Ummah. Buddhists cite examples such as the Five Precepts to inform their decision-making. Sometimes religious leaders do a better job of teaching family decision making than employers, schools or political organizations.

People in every country often cite their own examples of good or bad family leadership. In the last decade we have learned more about poor leadership skills as a result of global communication and social media than ever before. Look at Twitter. Look at Facebook. Look at political divisions, or even product reviews. Look at the evening "news." Or, you can turn those platforms off and talk directly to the important people in your life. Sometimes the best approach is to ignore those sources of outrage, and practice being a better leader in your family.

One way to start being a better leader is by answering this question: If you could have dinner tonight with anyone from any time or any place, who would it be and why?

Pause here.

Your answer describes what you value. I don't want to know the name or details of that dinner date. I *do* want to know what you value, because that informs your behavior. You may value family, business, politics, religion, celebrity, violence, wealth... Your answer indicates what I should say and do to develop a deeper relationship with you, as well as what I should *never* say or do.

I often use that question with leaders to encourage them to build trust with one another. If a 10-year old says, "I want to talk to Grandpa because he's dead now, but he always used to have good advice," then you know that wisdom is a value that will shape behavior in that family. Try asking that "dinner question" at your next family meeting or business meeting.

My experience is that all family leaders try to do their best. I've met thousands of parents, all of whom state, "I want my child to have a better life than my childhood." I spent nine years directing a non-profit program at a Quaker School near Washington, D.C. Our team of over 120 staff grew that program over 900% with over 3,500 children each year. They were the most culturally diverse independent school in the country; the parents and children came from every country in the world. Regardless of their origin, every parent had the same desire. All parents want the best opportunities for their children.

I also spent 12 years teaching over 2,500 young adults at 4 independent high schools, and once again I met thousands of parents. Every parent invested in their child for the same reason: they all wanted their child to have more opportunities than they did. In fact, many family leaders lacked leadership skills, and knew that their 16-year old child would have better opportunities if they went to an independent boarding school than if they remained at home with their parents.

> Family leaders, and family-owned business leaders, try their best, but lack leadership skills.

Family leaders lack leadership skills at micro levels, such as a nuclear family, and at a macro level as well. Consider how millions of people respond to global events, such as World Wars or refugee migration or diseases. From 1940 - 1945, in almost every country and culture, resources were redistributed so that young men (typically) could travel to distant lands to fight against other young men from other lands (typically). One impact of that global event was disruption in family leadership. Women took over new responsibilities in workplaces from Chicago to Berlin. Children worked on farms and factories at younger ages, for longer hours. Trillions of assets shifted from savings in real property to speculative virtual markets. Millions of people relocated from rural to urban areas. Billions of people re-married, divorced or became single parents.

None of those family leaders had a book chapter on OKR Leadership that provided any clarity for those disruptions. While family leaders in every culture may try their best to be more effective parents, there will never be one book on parenting. People are too complex, and there are too many situational variables (e.g., culture, religion, economics, politics). However, there are common guidelines and approaches that we can use despite these differences.

Family-owned business leaders try their best

The second problem this chapter addresses is the need for more family-owned business leaders to embrace OKR Leadership. When family members own at least 20% of the voting rights of a company, then that business may be listed as family-owned. As stated earlier in this chapter, over 70% of businesses in the U.S, are privately owned by family members who drive trillions of assets annually. Some of the world's largest family-owned businesses are publicly traded; examples in the U.S include Ford Motor Company, Comcast, and Walmart.

Family-owned businesses typically account for the majority of the wealth in *every* country and public financial index across the world. That distribution is mirrored in almost *every* business sector. For current details on family-owned businesses see Pew Foundation Reports, Forrester Research or Forbes listings. You may know many owners of family-owned businesses in agriculture, retail, or professional services. Those business leaders all struggle with limited time, money, and technology problems. That fact is not new, or limited to these kinds of businesses.

However, the access to validated processes for talent management solutions and succession management solutions for family-owned businesses *is* new. Over 60% of their working capital expenses are invested in people (e.g., salary, compensation, benefits) – and 100% of those people problems are manageable.

The Family Business Consulting Group (FBCG) is the leading business consultancy in the United States exclusively devoted to helping family enterprises prosper across generations. (Disclosure: I am delighted to be a FBCG consultant. See www.thefbcg.com and the chapter endnotes for details). For over 25 years, we have served over 2,500 client families in 70 countries. Our mission is "to help family businesses prosper across generations." Our expert consultant team has successfully led businesses, in countless industries and cultures, focus on their unique objectives and key results (e.g., succession planning, governance, communication, conflict resolution). As the managing director Drew Mendoza says, "We partner with each family business to deliver the solutions they require, with unmatched integrity and professionalism."

The market demand for family business consulting in the U.S. is enormous. As Jennifer Wilson, Director of PWC business services explained to me, if it were spun off as a separate company, the PWC business services group would be the fourth largest accounting consulting company in the U.S., behind Deloitte, PWC, Ernst & Young and above KPMG. Their primary market is family business leaders with assets over $10M. Those business leaders need the information contained in this chapter to discover how family business leaders can implement OKR Leadership and make better choices.

Family-owned business leader roles

One of my recent family-owned business clients is a great example of a company that's implementing OKR Leadership. Their fourth-generation retail business employees over 80 people. The third-generation owner has provided one non-voting share to each of his three adult children for distribution when he transfers ownership. Like many business owners, he is aged 65, tired, and worried about passing on the legacy of their family business.

He says, "I don't want to die with my boots on. I want these children to learn how to make decisions together that perpetuate our family history and provide outstanding customer service to our clients."

His wife and mother of their three children, shares his concern: "Frankly, I don't know how to help our family stay together. We raised our children to think independently but now there is so much conflict that we can't even have family dinners together. My fear is that we will be forced to sell the business and let them continue to fight with one another."

Their concerns reflect common research trends in family business leaders everywhere. Succession planning is often described as "the final test of greatness" for a family legacy. However, less than one-third of family businesses survive into the second generation, and only about 13% survive to the third generation. (See industry trends and publications at the Family Business Consulting Group or Family Firm Institute or chapter endnotes).[1]

In my client's company, each of their children worked in other industries for other employers so that they could learn from those other employers. When I was engaged to work with the family, the two youngest children were employed in the business. The middle child, age 32, was recently promoted to manage the national sales division, which generated over 50% of their gross revenue and represented over 70% of their strategic growth. The youngest child, age 27, was recently promoted from the retail sales floor to manage purchasing and procurement.

Shortly thereafter, the eldest child, age 36, was employed in the business as director of operations. He did so, in part, because his father (in his words), "Finally invested in a business psychologist to help our family develop the skills we need to lead this business."

The OKR Leadership process has provided new vocabulary words and a scalable process for countless family business leaders. I introduced this family to key vocabulary words such as "objectives," "key results," "manager," leader," because they frequently confused those terms. I introduced them to validated models of succession planning that included guidelines for their three overlapping roles as 1) family members, 2) managers, and 3) owners. I facilitated 12 family meetings that occurred every two to three weeks so that they could develop their guidelines or rules when interacting in each of those roles. When working with complex systems such as family-owned businesses, practicing leadership over time can be a critical variable for success.

I often use the image in Figure 6.0 to describe the complexity in family business leadership. The largest circle is the family, because the shared objective of *all* family members and non-family members is to enable the family-owned business to prosper across generations. Family members are born or married into that circle. Managers may or may not be family members. Owners are at least 20% family members. They each have different roles. Of course, one person may be in multiple circles.

Figure 6.0: Family-owned business leader roles

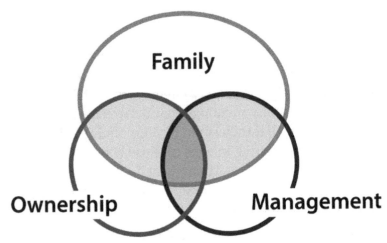

The next few pages share three scenarios that you can apply to your family-owned business, or to your consulting practice. These scenarios focus on succession planning, cost reduction and organizational change using OKR Leadership in family-owned businesses.

Succession planning leadership

The primary objective for the consulting engagement in this first scenario was to accelerate the process of transitioning the management and ownership of the business to the next generation of family business owners.

Key Results always vary in response to changing external variables. For instance, we agreed to these five key results when I began this engagement:

KR1: Assess the strengths, weaknesses, hidden talents and blind spots of all five nuclear family members using a series of 1:1 confidential interviews and validated assessments (e.g., the DISC, PIAV, VIA strengths, and EI assessments.) Distribute those team assessment results to the nuclear family members in a family meeting within 30 days.

KR2: Create a customized succession planning manual within the next six months that can be used as a reference manual for decades ahead.

KR3: Develop family rules for decision-making, key roles, schedules, milestones, timelines, managing conflict, evaluation, note taking and direct communication within the next three months. See the example in Figure 17 below.

KR4: Design and facilitate a series of up to 14 family business meetings in the next 12 months, if needed.

KR5: Design and facilitate a Family Council Meeting with advisors (e.g., attorneys, accountants, financial advisors, business mentors) and extended family members at some point within the next twelve months.

This client ended up deciding that they did not need to invest in KR5 because they had developed the spreadsheets and processes to facilitate a Family Council Meeting on their own. This client also determined after 12 (not 14) meetings that they had achieved the desired result of KR4. The client was delighted. I was delighted. Therefore this phase of our OKR Leadership consulting engagement was complete.

It may seem overwhelming, but role confusion can often be reduced. The process of conducting one on one consulting sessions with each of the family members helped me understand their concerns. That process also accelerated their trust in me. They each publicly stated their commitment to the OKR Leadership process. My role as a facilitator was to respect their confidentiality while addressing their shared concerns in a series of family meetings that were both productive and emotional. People are emotional. At one point some family members stood up and threatened to leave. At another time, there were tears and name calling. But there were statements of unselfish love and gratitude at many other moments. Over time, that family business leadership team developed clarity about each of the roles listed in Figure 17 below.

> Role confusion must be reduced
> in family-owned business leaders.

Figure 6.1 is a list from one team of family business leaders. You must develop your own list with skillful facilitation over time.

Figure 6.1: Sample family business leader roles

Rule:	Family:	Management:	Ownership:
Names	Use role 100% (father, brother, sister)	Use first names 100% all work-related activities	Use first names 100% of the time.
Gossip	Seek to understand. Listen. Model unselfish love.	Provide feedback to manager. Support other manager's decisions. Do not refer conflict to any third party.	After work hours, direct communication 100%. Avoid any triangulation.

Public behavior	Be vocally supportive of one another's strengths.	Be paragons of the best family values and be cautious. Focus on business outcomes in any social event. Publicly recognize good work from others.	Be seen as a team. Assume the best of others. Seek long term value. Recognize good work from others.
Communication	Use the complete communication wheel when useful to avoid conflict.	Use data/ big want/ wills. Avoid opinions/ feelings. Eliminate our social media presence.	Use the complete communication wheel 100% of time to foster good decision making.
Professionalism	Always support one another in public.	Always speak the truth. Always act with integrity. Publicly recognize good work from others.	Speak directly to others when potential for emotion or judgment or conflict
Roles	Support new roles by sharing expertise.	Always assume good will in others. Say "yes" if the recommendation supports our "One Family" business vision.	Maintain focus on the long-term value of our "One Family" business vision.
Decision making	Seek to understand needs of loved ones, then make decisions. Adopt the decision-making process we agreed to.	Use the importance screen to determine economic, strategic and stakeholder interests. Adopt the decision-making process we agreed to.	Solicit feedback from multiple stakeholders before making decisions. Adopt the decision-making process we agreed to.

Managing conflict	Seek to understand loved ones today, as unselfish adults.	Speak directly when potential for emotion or judgment or conflict	Speak directly when potential for emotion or judgment or conflict

OKR Leadership to reduce costs

The second scenario describes how a family can use OKR Leadership to save time, money and resources.

I received a referral from a third-generation family-owned business leader who said, "I have been fired five times and I have quit at least 6-7 times. My grandfather understands me, but my father and uncle do not understand my business decisions at all. They refuse to invest in technology or people. They refuse to fund my division. We are making money, but they are not. I need to learn how to work with them or I need to leave for good."

His frustrations are representative of countless family business leaders.

In the discovery assessment phase of this consulting engagement, the business founder, the grandfather, stated, "My grandson will no longer listen to any of us. He abuses people. He thinks he is the smartest person in every conversation. We don't know what to do with him."

The second-generation co-owners (brothers, who are the father and uncle) stated, "If he wants to work with a business psychologist, then we are willing to try anything." Their primary objective was to determine if they could define a role for the third generation family member, or determine if they would be forced to sell the business outside the family.

Assessments are critical for family business leaders when they have different objectives. In this example, the objective of the grandfather, father and uncle was to determine the business' future. The objective of the third-generation leader was to fight for additional resources. When family business leaders have different objectives, then there is likely to be conflict. Additionally, this particular family pattern included decades of verbal abuse. I started the engagement by conducting individual interviews with all four family business leaders. I required each leader to agree upon ground rules for effective communication, to help them break that pattern.

We then agreed to a series of facilitated family meetings designed to assess each family member's strengths, weaknesses, blind spots and hidden talents. I reviewed the ground rules designed to facilitate listening and effective communication at these family meetings. However, in the first 60-minute meeting, the third-generation leader spoke over 70% of the time and repeatedly accused the other members of bad judgement. I was unable to interrupt him despite repeated efforts to do so. Like a child who was displeased, he used the meeting to attack his father, uncle and grandfather.

The second meeting was rescheduled. I used this added time to conduct a series of individual video-based sessions with the third-generation leader so that he could see video recordings of his behavior. We discussed how there was no possibility of him achieving his desired objective if he did not permit others to speak at least 50% of the time. He agreed to a key result of reducing his speaking time from 70% to less than 50% of the time in their second meeting.

I used a timer to measure that KR in the second meeting, and he did indeed reduce the amount of time speaking from 70% to less than 50%. He also reduced the number of abusive adjectives, adverbs and judgements to fewer than 10 in that 60-minute meeting.

> OKR Leadership can be a useful tool for consultants using a behavior-based methodology.

The grandfather, father and uncle said, "That was the best meeting we have had together in over 20 years. We think he listened to us. We think he is capable of working for us in the future." They were more hopeful and optimistic than they had been in years. That is, they felt they had the "will and the way" to develop a better future, and a general positive affect or belief in a mutually beneficial outcome. (You may recall the discussion in chapter 3 about PsyCap, which includes measures of hope and optimism).

The third family meeting enabled these leaders to discuss one another's strengths for the first time in their lives. The grandfather, father and uncle shared historical context for business decisions made decades before, such as a Veterans Administration backed bank loan with a reduced interest rate that enabled them to purchase additional warehouses across the street. The third-generation leader shared stories of how technology accelerated marketing and sales from $50M to $70M in 12 months, and how regular performance review feedback increased employee retention over 30% in his division. While they still were not ready to have family dinners or vacations together, for the first time in their lives they shared stories about struggling to keep the business going for over 80 years. Those stories had never been shared because they had never been able to listen to one another before.

However, the fourth family meeting shattered their hopes, optimism and strength-building work to date when the third-generation leader declared, "I have decided that I hate manufacturing and I need to leave this business. I will help you find a successor to lead this division. But I am not willing to be a part of this family business."

That declaration surprised me. More importantly, that declaration surprised the first- and second-generation business leaders.

However, they each quickly accepted his declaration and discussed how to manage the transitional responsibilities. They finally had a clear future – even if it wasn't the objective that we'd originally been working toward. We discussed critical milestones for succession management. They each agreed to requirements for sharing client account information that had previously been withheld, vendor partner data that could no longer have restricted access, access to employee records that had previously been denied, and timelines for each milestone.

Personally, I was delighted because I had no more desire to work with that verbally abusive client any longer. The owners were delighted because they quickly achieved their objective of a clear future; they saved time and money using the OKR Leadership process.

Organizational change example

This third scenario of family-owned business leadership represents the need for organizational change in every business. Remember what we discussed in chapter 1 — all business leaders need to innovate or die.

This company's founder had struggled to create an internet-based retail business for 30 years. He has two sons, one of whom developed proprietary software. The other son developed operational efficiencies. Finally, after 25 years of struggles, their business exploded in growth five years ago. Revenue increased from $4M to over $16M in those five years. They suddenly realized that they needed to develop organizational maturity. After conducting assessments and defining their OKR Leadership process, I provided them with the model in Figure 18.

There are countless silly models marketed in the 20-year old discipline of organizational leadership. Be wary. This model in Figure 6.2 is based on validated research and my consulting practice.[2.] The phases of a pre-launch, launch, implementation and sustaining the change can be applied to any initiative at your team or organization. The old behaviors need to unfreeze, or melt away, like an ice cube into water, before the new behaviors can refreeze into the new initiative. My experience is that organizational change always requires a focus on new relationships and behaviors.

Figure 6.2: Organizational leadership that works

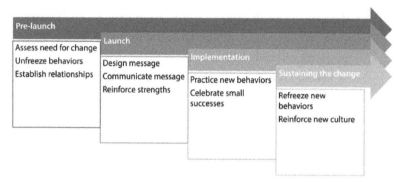

When I provided this model to the family, I asked, "What are you launching?"

They all agreed, "We need a technological system integrated with our warehouse operational system before Q3 so that we can meet the seasonal demands of Q4."

I said, "I understand your urgency. What systems have you written or developed that you can depend on?"

Their jaws dropped.

Like so many family-owned business leaders, they operated verbally. They modelled trust in one another. But they did not have *written operational* processes, job descriptions, contract agreements, performance reviews, or any measures of their efficiency, effectiveness or outcomes.

The main point of this example is that many family-owned business leaders operate this way: in unspoken assumptions or verbal agreements. But as businesses mature, they require written and digital processes to reinforce their new objectives.

Key points from Chapter 6, Family Leadership and OKR Leadership

1. The primary objective of this chapter is to define the problem of family leadership for family members, owners and consultants.
2. A secondary objective of this chapter is to provide examples of how you can apply OKR Leadership to a family-owned business
3. Family leaders try their best, but often lack leadership skills.
4. Family-owned business leaders also try their best, and require OKR Leadership to practice what matters next. Examples include succession planning, cost reduction and organizational change.

Key questions from Chapter 6, Family Leadership and OKR Leadership

1. Who are some of the best family leaders you know? What behaviors or values do they demonstrate that makes them so remarkable?
2. Family-owned business leaders often describe confusion about their overlapping roles as family members, managers and owners. Using Figures 17 and 18, how would you advise any family-owned business leaders to become more effective?
3. How can you apply OKR Leadership your family-owned business? Or in your family?

CHAPTER 7. WHAT'S NEXT?

Impact studies. Technology. Diversity. Positive Psychology. The OKR Leadership project 2020+.

Naturally, any chapter with a title like "What's next?" needs to be short, and provocative.

A book editor once told me that only 20% of book buyers read the last chapter. If you are one of those 20% then we are in the same nerdy camp together. Thank you for your persistence.

This chapter will discuss business and personal impact case studies, OKR software and technology, the trend toward diversity and inclusion, recent research in Positive Psychology, and an invitation to participate in the OKR Leadership project in 2020 and beyond.

There are no fortune cookies or tea leaves in this final chapter, but there is plenty of optimism and next steps for you to practice OKR Leadership in your career, team or organization.

Business Impact Case Study

In 2019, I conducted an OKR business impact case study using two randomly matched groups in the same F500 organization. The participants were 28 District Sales Managers (DSMs) in the U.S. and Canada. A Focus Group and a Control Group were created in 2017 to solicit feedback and provide specialized training. The result was a classic opportunity for a natural business impact case study. In May, 2019, I provided a 4-hour OKR Leadership training program for the Focus Group. The Control Group did not receive that training. All other business expectations were matched and identical, according to their manager.

Pause here.

Would you expect that any 4-hour training on any topic would have a significant measurable impact on business measures?

The results of this 4-hour OKR Leadership training program for the Focus Group were significant. We measured monthly data before the focus group training from January to May (Time 1), and after the training from June to September (Time 2). Then we measured monthly data for the control group from January to September. The monthly measures included total revenue, gross margins as a percentage of revenue, deviations, EBITDA, and specific business lines. The business impact difference was over 4%.

The client was so encouraged by these results that they requested a second OKR training program for all DSMs in the Focus Group and Control Group. In September, 2019, four months later, I provided a 2-hour training to all 28 DSMs. Those results will be measured monthly, and are not yet available as this book goes to press in October, 2019.

I strongly recommend that you replicate this natural business impact case study design. Create two randomly matched groups (i.e., by job title, geography, key variables such as new managers or high potential employees). Determine the business metrics that you need to measure. Provide OKR Leadership training to one group (Or hire us to do so.) Then measure your business impact. The data should recommend your next actions. If you have questions, contact me at www.Action-Learning.com or use the resource links in chapter 8.

Personal Impact Case Study

The above example for a team can also be applied at a personal level. Consider whatever you are measuring today. When I start meetings I often ask, "What are you measuring?" as a way to quickly get everyone on board. I call them GOB questions. Examples of those measurements range from "my daily calories and exercise" to "my personal net worth" to "the number of days until vacation." The specific answers are less important than this fact: We *all* require measures to track our objectives.

Here are some personal examples designed to provoke you to measure *your* OKRs. One of my objectives is to model profitability for my loved ones. For decades I have posted a balance sheet on my office door. That balance sheet lists revenue and expenses monthly, and is updated quarterly. Occasionally I have short meetings with my family to discuss cash flow or possible investments. One result of posting those balance sheets is that our adult children are now more aware of small business risk and profitability. I also post a list of "Passionate Actions" that I am excited about in each calendar year. Those actions include family trips, personal trips, conferences, big project due dates, big investments. The result of posting those actions is that my family members see what I am excited about, and how my consulting business supports my objective of providing for my family.

Personal examples from my clients do not always directly relate to business; they often relate to diet, exercise and health. If one of your objectives is to reduce weight, then your caloric intake and regular exercise should be a KR. Accountability with positive influences (i.e., diet partners, gym partners, supportive loved ones) should be a KR. Avoidance of negative influences (i.e., drugs, alcohol, unsupportive people) should be a KR. You can apply the OKR Leadership examples in this book to any individual objective, as discussed in chapter 5.

One of my 45-year old business clients struggled so much with diet and exercise that he said, "My obesity is a career limitation." His objective was to lose 120 pounds and keep the weight off for five years. He astounded many of his colleagues when he lost that 120 pounds — with professional support from a registered dietician — in less than 9 months. He has kept the weight off for two years so far, and he regularly tells me how many months and days have passed since he met his weight goal. His KR2 was subjective well-being — he felt like a winner and wanted to retain that feeling. His KR3 was that he modelled personal transformation when speaking to others. And in due time he was promoted in his career. My experience is that our bodies are like temples that require ongoing reverence and maintenance. Sadly, some people take better care of their cars than they do their own health and well-being.

Whatever you measure is critically important to your impact as a leader.

Here is a testimonial from one of my clients, a plant manager: "I am using OKR Leadership to align my team on essential business needs. As a result, we are over $520,000 in the black this year and I'm on track for a 60% bonus of $65,000. If our team stays focused on our OKRs, then my family may get out of debt by the end of the year."

What is your OKR Leadership testimonial?

TIPS for writing your OKR testimonial

1. Write quantitative measures (numbers) for your personal and business impact case study.
2. Use any current measures to create a baseline, like any athlete. Add qualitative measures (how you feel or think) if useful.
3. Select a positive accountability partner and ask for their regular support.
4. Track your data over 6 months. Share the data regularly with your accountability partner or coach. Use a video recording monthly to track your changes over time.
5. Assess your data and make recommendations to guide your future behavior.

Technology

The global impact of technology on our careers, teams and organizations cannot be overstated.[1] Humans have always depended upon technology for survival and collaboration. When over 40% of the global population (2.4 billion people) use one social media platform called Facebook for "news" or "connection to others," the impact is tremendous. When over 300 million Amazon customers have global digital access to this OKR Leadership book, the potential impact on your team and organization is huge. When over 51% of your team or organization is tracking OKRs the impact may be transformative.

There are several technology providers offering customized software to accelerate OKR leadership. Here are a few examples to illustrate the depth of choices for you. I strongly recommend that you vet these technology vendors with care, using a short list of required and recommended features for your team or organization.

Betterworks software is based on John Doerr's book, *Measure What Matters,* and he is on their advisory board. They have a strong reputation with larger organizations. Atiim has a strong reputation with smaller organizations. 15Five has roots in positive psychology and has a strong reputation with technology companies. For contacts in these three organizations please contact me directly.

To be clear, you may not need to invest in any additional technology to support your OKR leadership initiatives. Paper and pencils may be sufficient technology. My clients are using Google Docs, Microsoft Teams, Jabber, Slack, PowerPoint, SharePoint, WebEx, Zoom, Skype, GoToMeeting, merged phone calls, photos, video recordings, posters, and notes on yellow legal pads or Postix. The main point is to use any available technology to support your OKR leadership initiatives. Practice leadership.

One of my clients said it best, "OKR leadership is like playing football. I don't care how our offense scores points, but they just need to show me the results."

Diversity and inclusion

The competitive advantages of diversity and inclusion in your team or organization cannot be ignored, and can be designed into your OKRs. In response to income and social inequality, the Ford Foundation recently published a "new gospel" to measure stakeholder capitalism and social value of companies. Ethical leadership and diversity can be measured and ranked, as described at Ethisphere, Just Capital, and the Global Impact Investing Network.

I strongly encourage you to review these trends, and then send your OKR Leadership examples to me as described below in the OKR Leadership Project for 2020.

Consider your reaction to these points:

1. When women and people from diverse backgrounds, including key customer segments, are included on the boards of publicly traded companies, those companies have higher shareholder value than those with less diverse board composition.
2. Artificial intelligence algorithms are designed to minimize racism by reducing hiring bias for people who "look like the hiring managers".
3. Amazon is automating their hiring process because their 40% year over growth rate and demand for diversity of new employees requires that they eliminate the inefficiency of including people in the hiring process.
4. The CEO of HireVue states that the accuracy of hiring software, based on video, audio and written responses using 120 data points, enables any organization or diversity initiative to attract the most qualified, most diverse population possible.
5. Global migrations of immigrants to Canada support their objective of attracting over 25% more people annually, to support their increased needs for a culturally, racially, economically and socially diverse population.
6. The explosion of diverse perspectives and contradictory statements on social media platforms such as Twitter and Instagram have catalyzed political and social objectives such as national elections, Brexit, the Arab Spring in 2010-2012, and the Hong Kong protests in 2019.

The question for you is, how are you including diversity in your OKR Leadership?

Positive Psychology

I believe that we are on the cusp of a moral sea change in organizational leadership that demands ethical behavior and transparent leadership. Leaders – just like you — can practice OKR leadership using the model of positive psychology for both direction and accountability. Let me explain.

Positive Psychology (PP) is defined as art and science of well-being. An academic definition of PP is the scientific pursuit of optimal human functioning and applied interventions that leverage human strengths[2.] Typical research questions include "What makes life meaningful?" and "How can practitioners foster well-being and optimal functioning?" In 1998, several leading psychologists looked at the published research and asked, "Why are 65% of the published papers focusing on mental illness?" In response to that imbalance, they said, "Let's focus on mental health, the other half of human behavior." Subsequent research clustered around five categories or themes, which can be described using the acronym PERMA (i.e., positive emotions, engagement, relationships, meaning, and accomplishment)[3]. Let me explain each.

Positive emotions

The P in PERMA stands for positive emotions. Negative emotions (e.g., fear, anger, sadness) alert us to potential dangers, therefore they are critical for our survival and adaptation to threats. In contrast, positive emotions signal safety and our response is to broaden and build upon them for the future. All emotions trigger physiological changes (e.g., heart rate, pupil dilation, skin temperature, oxytocin, muscle tension). The broaden and build theory states that positive emotions broaden your psychological and behavioral repertoires and build your psychological resources. The top ten positive emotions are: love, joy, gratitude, serenity/contentment, interest, hope, pride, amusement, inspiration, and awe[4]. In fact, if you read that list out loud you may shift your emotional state in a millisecond.

The question becomes how much should OKR leaders reinforce positive emotions? They are subjective, change throughout the day and change throughout one's lifetime. The short answer is to practice both direction and accountability. Direction is easy to assess. When you ask others, "How are you feeling?" you must stop – drop – and — listen carefully, then acknowledge the other person accurately. When you ask others, "How can I help you?" they may not be able to answer, but they will know that you are modelling empathy, the greatest predictor of well-being.

Engagement

The E in the PERMA model stands for engagement or flow. What happens when you are fully engaged in a familiar activity, such as reading a book or hitting golf balls? Typically, you experience tension between the degree of challenge and the degree of skill. When the challenge is high and the skill is low, you feel anxiety. When the skill is high and the challenge is low, you feel boredom. When there is a balance between skill and challenge, time seems to stand still. Work is easy. That state of optimal balance is called the Flow State. The physiology of flow can be measured (e.g., quicker response to stimuli, balanced adrenal levels, subjective feeling fully of capability)[5]. A familiar example for leaders is that nervous energy you experience just prior to an important meeting, which may help you to find the right words or choose the best behavior (e.g., patterns in prefrontal cortex choices, mirror neuron activity). In short, engagement requires that you make smart choices.

The question becomes, what is the balance between your skill and challenge? For instance, if you spend hours analyzing spreadsheet data instead of assessing worker satisfaction levels, then you may be engaged in the wrong activities. Most leaders know that diet and exercise are critical for good health, but that does not mean that you are making good choices about diet and exercise. Similarly, most leaders know that they need to develop others. But how many use an accountability partner to help manage the leadership development of their work groups or teams? When leaders like you choose to move from awareness (e.g., reading this chapter) to actions that foster engagement in your work teams (e.g., discussing this chapter), then you are more likely to demonstrate accountability. As stated above, practicing OKR leadership requires that you practice two critical elements: direction and accountability.

Relationships

The R in the PERMA model stands for an objective assessment on the quality and quantity of your relationships. A provocative question is, "How many people can you call at 2:00 a.m. to ask for help?" Those people may be your closest friends, your inner circle, and they are critical for your well-being. In my OKR leadership workshops I frequently ask people to list the top 6 stakeholders in their business life. Then list the top 6 stakeholders in your personal life. Those 12 people are critical relationships for you. Most workshop participants cannot list 12 stakeholders. You may need to add names to your list. Perhaps you know that social isolation is rampant in the U.S., at all age levels and all economic levels, and is highly correlated with anxiety, depression and mental illness. You need to nurture close personal relationships, with at least 12 stakeholders of supportive people, today.

Here is another activity that I often do in workshops that demonstrates the need for relationships. Imagine that two leaders are randomly paired up and given a simple task. Leader #1 must look in another's eyes for 7 seconds. Leader #2 must not show any emotional response, smile, or avert their eyes. My experience is that over 75% of all audiences are not able to control their response for 7 seconds. This short activity illustrates a universal truth about what it means to be human. We are social animals, therefore our relationships matter. Actors practice this activity. Leaders like you can practice developing better relationships with the key 12 stakeholders in your OKR success. The most effective way to build those relationship is to express gratitude for others, daily.

Meaning

The M in the PERMA model stands for meaning or purpose. Two key questions include, "What will make today meaningful?" and "Who can I help today?" My experience is that if you can answer those two questions, then you have a strong sense of meaning in your life. If you cannot answer those two questions, then you need to increase meaning in your life. Pick something significant to stand for. Place a stake in a sandy beach. Declare what is important to you. If you need more meaning in your world, then you may need a bigger meaning, or a bigger flagpole with a bigger flag. Our cultural biases affect meaning. Western philosophers since Aristotle have stated that reason makes life meaningful; Eastern philosophers since Buddha have stated that acceptance of harmony and balance makes life meaningful. Researchers in the U.S. seem to focus on meaning in love and work.

Here is an activity that demonstrates your focus on meaningful work. Imagine three buckets. Each bucket describes your perspective about work, as described in chapter 5. Label the first bucket either a job, a career, or a calling. Then write one example of what that label means to you. For instance, if your perspective about work is that work is a career, then one associated perspective is that you work to provide for loved ones. A second perspective is that your career decisions are related. A third perspective is that your career will change 10 times. Then repeat that process 7-8 times, to determine 7-8 different, deeper perspectives that explore what meaningful work means to you. Then pick the most meaningful perspective. The label — whatever it was — has not changed. But your understanding of its meaning has changed. Oftentimes my clients shift their behavior when they quit stating "My perspective about work is ___" and start saying "Work can be more meaningful for me if ___." In other words, practicing leadership requires both direction and accountability.

Accomplishment

The A in the PERMA models stands for accomplishment, one of the central assumptions of this OKR Leadership book. Your objectives describe what you intend to accomplish. Researchers describe different types of accomplishments, such as the need for achievement, power or affiliation. You may measure your professional accomplishments (e.g., projects, behavioral or performance objectives, rewards), or your personal accomplishments (e.g. hobbies, diet and exercise, net worth, celebrations, or that vacation trip to Hawaii). In the U.S., researchers describe a positivity bias that drives people to pursue happiness, called subjective well-being.

Researchers disagree on the percentages, but genetics and environment are key variables in the pursuit of happiness. Here is another personal example. When I was in graduate school, at Dartmouth College, in the 1990s, I was taught that happiness resulted from a 50-50 balance between genetics /nature and environment/ nurture. In response, I decided to quit researching unhappy topics, like mental illness, anxiety or depression. I spent the next 25 years in applied psychology, as a teacher, leadership consultant, executive coach, helping people control their actions and thoughts so that they could attain whatever professional or personal goals they desired. Thankfully, when I resumed my formal research, as a doctoral student, in 2014, I learned that the science of Positive Psychology had caught up to my applied experiences and wisdom from others.

The science of accomplishments suggests that about 40% of your capacity for happiness is defined by a "set point" of individual choices for how you think and how you act[6.] Your genetic predisposition may explain about 50%. And your external circumstances (e.g., a windfall or tragedy) may explain the remaining 10%. The central point for you and your accomplishments is profound: you have the capacity to determine conditions for about 40% of your happiness. Practicing leadership requires direction and accountability. You may be expert at creating lists, sharing accountability goals, and rewarding accomplishments. Most people need to practice. Here is a simple activity that promotes accomplishment and reinforces your 40% set point. Select one of the happiest or most successful people you know. Imitate their actions and thoughts for a day. Express gratitude to that person. Express kindness to at least five people daily. Write down at least five things you are grateful for. Then continue those activities for a week and study the effect of your new actions and thoughts. What did you notice?

The goal of any leadership development model is to mirror reality. For instance, if *you* adopt the assumption that OKR leaders like *you* have the capacity to grow into your unique potential as an expert leader, then leadership outcomes such as positive psychology become attainable. Well-being requires you to embrace a growth mindset. The PERMA model of positive emotions, engagement, relationships, meaning and accomplishments provides a useful framework to mirror the reality of leadership development.

The OKR Leadership Project 2020

Here is my invitation for YOU to join the OKR Leadership Project.

The goal of the OKR leadership project is to invite practitioners/ leaders/ managers in any-sized organization to share testimonials of HOW you are applying OKRs in your career, team or organization.

What are the assumptions of the OKR Leadership project?

1. Leaders must practice leadership. We can all be better leaders.
2. We can leverage technology to share stories of how OKR leadership can transform careers, individuals and teams.
3. When we share testimonials, then we increase awareness and learning for other individuals and teams.

Frequently asked questions

Who can contribute to the OKR Leadership project? Anyone using the English language.

Why host the OKR Leadership project? After consulting hundreds of leaders and managers about OKR leadership one theme stands clear: using OKRs is NOT well defined. Market confusion and sloppy practices abound. This OKR Leadership Project is one initiative to help anyone at any level describe HOW you are applying OKRs individually and organizationally in our global marketplace. We need to share testimonials.

How do I contribute to the OKR Leadership process?

(a) share this invitation broadly with other OKR practitioners and colleagues

(b) schedule a 30-minute session with Doug Gray at https://www.action-learning.com/ on the blog

(c) receive the calendar confirmation link and reserve that time in your calendar,

(d) prepare your responses to the 5-6 questions below,

(e) download https://zoom.us/ software and learn how to use Zoom software using tutorials from YouTube, if needed,

(f) at our scheduled time, Doug will record 5-10 minutes of our video session

(g) Doug will send your MP4 recording to you for your distribution,

(h) Doug may post our recording in the OKR leadership project video or book series

What are the questions asked in the OKR Leadership conversation?

1. Self-introduction: Who are you, what do you do, where are you located, do you have a website or invitation to share with others?

2. Definition: OKR leadership can be defined as a management methodology that helps people focus activity on the same important issues throughout an

organization. Some people focus on internal teams (small or large, formal or informal), some people are external practitioners, and some people focus on self-development. How do you typically define OKR leadership?

3. Interests: What attracts you to the science or practice of OKR leadership?
4. Clients: Who do you typically serve in your OKR leadership work? Please share 2-3 of your examples/ case studies/ successful experiences applying objectives and key results.
5. Trends: What trends or market opportunities do you see in the future for OKR leadership, technology or management consulting?
6. Referrals: Who else can you refer who (a) is applying OKR leadership with others and (b) may be willing to be included in this OKR leadership project?

Can I send you an article or video testimonial instead? Yes of course, in English.

When can I contribute? At any time. Calendar years in northern hemispheres adopt January 1 as a date for reinvention, annual goal setting, and preparation for the long cold winter. I have adopted October 1 as a better date for you to develop your new year. Your OKR Leadership year can begin at any time.

When does the contribution phase end? In Q4 of 2020 I intend to publish a collection of your OKR Leadership 2020 stories. If useful, it may be an annual event, like the Chicken Soup book series or the Winners Circle book series for wealth advisors. I want you to practice OKR Leadership.

Thank you in advance for your participation in the OKR Leadership 2020 project.

Leaders practice leadership, so let's get started.

Here's to you, at your best...

CHAPTER 8. RESOURCES.

Endnotes. Key points and questions. Fact sheet. Glossary.
Quiz. Digital resources. References.

ENDNOTES

Endnotes for chapter 1, Introduction to OKR Leadership

1. See Nevin, P.R. & Lamorte, Ben. (2016). *Objectives and Key Results; Driving Focus, Alignment and Engagement with OKRs.* Wiley; Hoboken, NJ. On June, 2019, that title in Amazon book sales ranked #291 in Business & Organizational Learning, #227 in Strategy & Competition, and #464 in Strategic Business Planning.

2. For 12 case studies and dramatic examples see John Doerr's best seller (2019) *Measure What Matters; How Google, Bono and the Gates Foundation Rock the World with OKRs.* Portfolio/Penguin, New York. I have purchased copies of this book for clients because it is easy to read and validated by Doerr's venture capitalism from Kleiner Perkins in Amazon, Google, Intuit, Netscape, Twitter and others. The Google Paybook in the appendix is well worth replicating in your career, team or organization.

3. See details in Girard, B. (2009). *The Google Way; How one company is revolutionizing management as we know it.* No Starch Press; San Francisco, CA. Some fiscal impact examples are in Schmidt, E. (2019). *Trillion Dollar Coach: The Leadership Playbook of Silicon Valley's Bill Campbell.* Harper Business: New York. On June, 2019, Amazon book sales overall #582 in Books, #2 in Business Mentoring & Coaching category, #22 in Business Management category, #36 in Business Leadership category. For an academic reference see Steiber, A. & Alange, S. (2013). "A corporate system for continuous innovation: the case of Google Inc." *European Journal of Innovation and Management, 16*(2), 243-264.

4. I often cite and give copies of this book to others. I strongly recommend Seligman, M.E.P. (2011) *Flourish; A Visionary New Understanding of Happiness and Well-Being.* Atria; New York. Marty Seligman is described as a grandfather and patron of Positive Psychology, and a generous leader. I've met him twice at conferences and I have asked him about my research and trends in the field. I regard him as one of the most influential mentors in my career.

5. See Dan Pink's best-seller (2009, 2011) *Drive: The Surprising Truth About What Motivates Us.* Riverhead; New York. Pink defines three variables for knowledge workers: mastery, autonomy and purpose (MAP). Note that these three variables are not unique to knowledge workers in technology organizations. I recall consulting a safety leader at a new nuclear construction site (while wearing steel-toed boots and a hard hat). We used the MAP framework for the leader to design a simple handwritten spreadsheet on a clipboard with a yellow pad of paper. The leader quickly assessed his direct reports, then determined what he needed to say or do to manage each of his direct reports. For a similar summary of intrinsic motivation traits see David McClelland's research on the need for affiliation, achievement and power.

6. For an academic discussion of 11 perspectives see *Theories of Small Groups, Interdisciplinary Perspectives* (2005). Poole, M.S. & Hollingshed, A.B., Eds. Sage Publications, Thousand Oaks, CA. Great models that mirror many disciplines.

7. See Seligman (2011).

8. See Doerr (2018).

Endnotes for Chapter 3, Why Use OKR Leadership?

1. The impact of a 90-minute web-based training program is described at Luthans, F., Avey, J. B., & Patera, J. L. (2008). Experimental Analysis of a Web-Based Training Intervention to Develop Positive Psychological Capital. *Academy of Management Learning & Education, 7(2)*, 209-221.

2. Sales outcomes are described in Friend, S.B., Johnson, J.S., Luthans, F. & Sohi, R.S. (2016). Positive psychology in sales; Integrating psychological capital. *Journal of Marketing Theory and Practice (24)*, 3, 306-327.

3. The competitive advantages of PsyCap are introduced and described in Luthans, F., Youssef-Morgan, C.M. & Avolio, B.J. (2007). *Psychological capital; Developing the human competitive edge.* Oxford, England; Oxford University Press. That research was expanded and deepened in their next book, Luthans, F., Youssef-Morgan, C.M. & Avolio, B.J. (2015). *Psychological capital and beyond.* Oxford, England; Oxford University Press. Applications to Health PsyCap and other related variables are also described in Luthans, F., Youssef, C. M., Sweetman, D. S., & Harms, P. D. (2013). Meeting the leadership challenge of employee well-being through relationship PsyCap and Health PsyCap. *Journal of Leadership & Organizational Studies, 20(1)*, 118-133.

4. In my research, aggregated PsyCap scores did not change significantly during a 3-month experimental period. There was no training designed to increase PsyCap scores for either group A or group B, so I did not expect them to change. One limitation of my research was that individual PsyCap scores could not be linked to individual

coaches, compliance levels or specific protocols. See the details at Gray, D.W. (2018). Dissertation: *Positive Psychology Coaching Protocols; Creating Competitive Advantage for Leader Development.* ProQuest; Ann Arbor, MI.

5. See endnote 3 for details. The PsyCap-12 assessment is available with permission from Mind Garden. Longer validated assessments are also available.

6. See the details on competitive advantages from my globally validated research published at Gray, D.W. (2018). Dissertation: *Positive Psychology Coaching Protocols; Creating Competitive Advantage for Leader Development.* ProQuest; Ann Arbor, MI.

7. The confusion in leadership development is described in all of these titles. *The end of leadership,* by Kellerman (2012) at Harvard, or *Leadership BS; Fixing workplaces and careers one truth at a time*, by Pfeffer (2015) at Stanford. For examples of confusion in talent management I recommend *The Talent Delusion; Why Data not intuition is the key to unlocking human potential,* by Chamorro-Premuzic (2017) at Hogan, and *Nine Lies about work; A freethinking leader's guide to the real world*, by Buckingham and Goodall (2019).

Endnotes for Chapter 4. How do I practice OKR Leadership?

1. One of the leaders in growth mindset research is Dweck, C.S. (2006). *Mindset; The new psychology of success.* New York: Random House. There is related research in an "outward mindset" and "servant leadership" that has been applied to schools, governments, businesses and families.

2. I met Fred Kiel at a conference in 2016 and we had a lively conversation about collecting data from CEOs. His research is broad and rigorous. I strongly recommend his book Kiel, F. (2015). *Return on character: The real reason leaders and their companies win.* Boston: Harvard Business Review Press.

Endnotes for Chapter 5, OKR Leadership and career development

1. See research in Wrzesniewski, A., McCauley, C. R., Rozin, P., & Schwartz, B. (1997). Jobs, careers, and callings: People's relations to their work. *Journal of Research in Personality 31*(1), 21-33. A summary is at Barnett, (2012). *Making Your Job More Meaningful.* Harvard Business Review; Cambridge, MA. For related research on physician burnout see Dyrbye, L. N., Varkey, P., Boone, S. L., Satele, D. V., Sloan, J. A., & Shanafelt, T. D. (2013). Physician satisfaction and burnout at different career stages. *Mayo Clinic Proceedings, 88*, 12, 1358-67.

2. See fascinating research on job crafting associated with the University of Michigan. One resource is Wrzesniewski, A., LoBuglio, L., Dutton, J.E. and Berg, J.M. (2013). Job crafting and cultivating positive meaning and identity in work. *Advances in Positive Organizational Psychology,1*, 281–302. See related research at Kashdan, T. B., & Steger, M. F. (2007). Curiosity and pathways to well-being and meaning in life: Traits, states, and everyday behaviors. *Motivation and Emotion*, 31, 159–17.

3. For historical reviews on work, and an integrated model, see Blustein, D. L. (2006). *The psychology of working: A new perspective for career development, counseling and policy.* New York: Routledge.

4. The psychology of work literature typically looks at traits that increase productivity, or vocational opportuni-

ty. Most industrial organizational (I/O) psychology focuses on how to maximize the productivity of others. One integrative, inclusive model is described by Super, D.E. (1957). *The psychology of careers.* New York: Harper & Row.

5. For predictions see Oppenheimer, A. (2019). *The robots are coming; The future of jobs in the age of automation.* Vintage; New York. For a general review see Waddill, D.D. & Marquardt, M.J. (2011). *The E-HR Advantage; The complete handbook for technology-enabled human resources.* Nicholas Brealey; Boston.

6. One of my good friends, John Mattox, has written two books on talent analytics and I highly recommend each of them. See Fitz-Enz, J. & Mattox, J.R. (2014). *Predictive analytics for human resources.* Wiley: Hoboken, NJ. See Mattox, J.R. & Van Buren, M. (2016). *Learning analytics; Measurement innovations to support employee development.* Kogan Page; London. For a critical view on talent I strongly recommend Chamorro-Premuzic, T. (2017). *The talent delusion; Why data, not intuition, is the key to unlocking human potential.* Piatkus; London. For a provocative view on career and talent I also recommend Buckingham, M. & Goodall, A. (2019). *Nine lies about work; A freethinking leaders guide to the real world.* Harvard Business Review; Boston.

Endnotes for Chapter 6, Family leadership and OKR Leadership

1. Family-owned business consulting requires expertise in system theory and organizational leadership. For evidence-based practices I strongly recommend the Family Business Group Publications series of 22 titles published by Palgrave Macmillan. I have given clients copies of *Fam-*

ily Business Succession; The final test of greatness (2011) and *Siblings and the family business; Making it work for business, the family, and the future* (2012). For consultants I recommend *Working with family businesses; A guide for professionals* (1996) by Bork, D., Jaffe, D.T., Lane, S.H., Dashew, L., & Heisler, Q.G. They are all luminaries, and David Bork is generous in conversation.

2. After years of research I developed the model in Figure 13. This model is adapted from two prolific scholars: Burke at Columbia and Kotter at Harvard. Burke, W.W. (2014). *Organizational Change; Theory and Practice, 4th ed.* Sage Publications; Los Angeles and Kotter, J.P. (1996). *Leading change.* Harvard Business School Press; Boston. I encourage you to use it with your team or organization.

Endnotes for Chapter 7, What's next?

1. The impact of technology on our workforce is terrifying many employees who fear that they will lose their jobs. And technology has always accelerated productivity and transformed countless industries. Here are several of my favorite new, well-written provocative books. For the economic impact of artificial intelligence, see *Prediction Machines; The simple economics of artificial intelligence* (2018), by Agrawal, A., Gans, J. and Goldfarb, A. Harvard Business Review Press, Boston. For an entertaining broad view of automation in the workforce see *The Robots are Coming; The future of jobs in the age of automation* (2019). Oppenheimer, A. Vintage, New York. For a dark view see *World without Mind; The existential threat of big tech* (2018). Foer, F. Penguin, New York. For an even darker view, see *The Age of Surveillance Capitalism; The fight for a human future at the new frontier of power* (2019). Zuboff, S. Hachette, New York. For examples from Accenture, see *Pivot to the Future, Discovering value and*

creating growth in a disrupted world (2019). Abbosh, O., Nunes, P. and Downes, L. Hachette, New York.

2. See the details on positive psychology from my research. Gray, D.W. (2018). Dissertation: *Positive Psychology Coaching Protocols; Creating Competitive Advantage for Leader Development.* ProQuest; Ann Arbor, MI. Gray

3. See Seligman, M.E.P. (2011). *Flourish; A visionary new understanding of happiness and well-being.* New York: Atria.

4. See Fredrickson, B.L. (2009). *Positivity; Top-notch research reveals the upward spiral that will change your life.* New York: Three Rivers Press and Fredrickson, B. L. (2013). Updated thinking on positivity ratios. *American Psychologist, 68,* 814-822.

5. See Csikszentmihalyi, M. (1990). *Flow: The Psychology of Optimal Experience.* New York: Harper and Row.

6. See Lyubomirsky, S. (2007). *The how of happiness; A practical guide to getting the life you want.* London, England: Piatkus.

KEY POINTS AND QUESTIONS BY CHAPTER

Key points from chapter 1, Introduction to OKR Leadership

1. **Objectives and Key Results (OKRs)** is a management methodology that helps people focus activity on the same important issues throughout their organization.
2. **Objectives** describe what you want to do. They are qualitative and subjective. Examples of objectives include "Increase revenue" or "Reduce undesired turnover."
3. **Key Results (KRs)** are the measures of each objective. They are quantitative and measurable. Examples include "increase recurring client sales revenue from $500K/month to $525K/month by the end of Q3" or "increase 1:1 performance reviews by 8% at all warehouses within 30 days."
4. **Leadership** is defined as influencing others' behavior toward a better future. The primary skill of effective leaders is public optimism.
5. Leaders practice leadership because it is challenging and critical for humanity.
6. People are both aspirational and confused.
7. You are capable of practicing OKR Leadership today.

Key questions from chapter 1, Introduction to OKR Leadership

1. What is one objective for your career, team or organization?
2. What are 3-4 key results that you could use to measure that objective?
3. How could OKR Leadership address the problems your organization is facing?
4. What could be the ultimate goal of practicing OKR Leadership in your organization?
5. How could implementing OKR Leadership benefit you or your loved ones?

Key points from Chapter two, What is OKR Leadership?

1. **OKR Leadership** is a process for managers and leaders to practice what matters.
2. **Objectives and key results (OKRs)** is a management methodology that helps companies focus effort on the same important issues throughout their organization
3. **Objectives** describe what you want to do. They are qualitative and subjective.
4. **Key results (KRs)** are the 3-5 measures of each objective. They are quantitative and measurable.
5. **KR Formula #1:** Adopt the formula "as measured by" to confirm if something is a good OKR.
6. **KR Formula #2:** Adopt the formula "from x to y by z date" when writing KRs. It will force you to use numbers, and model transparency.

Key questions from chapter 2, What is OKR Leadership?

1. Have all of your team members written their OKRs?
2. Have you distributed OKRs for your organization or team?
3. How are you implementing OKRs in your business? (e.g., decision-making, performance management, bonus rewards, career development, individual development plans, or talent assessments.)
4. How are you implementing OKRs in your productivity measures? (e.g., effectiveness, efficiency, behavior outcomes or performance outcomes.)
5. To what extent are you using OKRs to drive your business? To what extent do you think OKRs will drive your future business?
6. What OKR resources do you need to locate?
7. Add your questions here...

Key points from chapter 3, Why use OKR Leadership?

1. OKR Leadership is a process for managers and leaders to practice what matters.
2. You do not need to use OKR Leadership if your business is exceeding all performance expectations (but odds are, it isn't).
3. Businesses either grow or die in response to customer feedback. There is nothing in the middle.
4. People are hierarchical, aspirational and confused. Every organization aspires to improve the state of its members.

5. People require feedback. Feedback is how managers and leaders interact with others to maximize their performance. The best feedback process for OKR Leadership is the AD-FIT™ process, which I'll describe in chapter 4.

Key questions from chapter 3, Why use OKR Leadership?

1. What are the top 3-4 OKRs that the executive leaders in your organization use?
2. How is your team or organization staying focused on your KR metrics (not milestones or tasks)?
3. How are you rationalizing your investment in OKR Leadership to your executives, champions, buyers, consumers, and clients?
4. Since practicing OKRs in your team or organization, what changes have you measured to date?
5. Since practicing OKRs in your team or organization, what new behavior or performance outcomes do you hope to measure?
6. Regarding the Leadership Trust Index (LTI): to what extent do you trust the leaders in your organization? (score from 1 low to 10 high) and why?
7. Regarding the Follower Trust Index (FTI): to what extent do you think others in your organization trust you? (score from 1 low to 10 high) and why?

Key points from Chapter 4, How do you practice OKR Leadership?

1. Coaching is the primary skill managers practice to maximize others' productivity.
2. Managers and leaders can use the globally validated AD-FIT™ coaching process to provide feedback. The AD-FIT™ process is an evidence-based approach to positive psychology coaching or consulting based upon (a) awareness of strengths and growth mindset, (b) defining a meaningful objective or OKRs, (c) focus on the client's agenda, (d) interventions and interaction, (e) takeaways, and (f) percentage of compliance to this model. Trademarked and globally validated by Action Learning Associates, LLC, 2018.
3. You need to practice asking great questions, especially those that begin with "what" and "how." I use the OKR Pulse Survey question to measure adoption and organizational change over time. That question is, "To what extent are you using OKR Leadership to drive your business?" Score from 1 (low) to 10 (high).
4. You need to practice writing and sharing your OKRs. This is a public management approach designed to solicit feedback, model accountability and achieve outcomes.
5. You can make certain that your OKRs align with the mission, vision and strategy of your team or organization. People always create "order" out of chaos.
6. I recommend that you review your OKRs quarterly. OKRs are a feedback process that ALL colleagues require.

Key questions from chapter 4, How do you practice OKR Leadership?

1. Use the OKR Pulse Survey Question regularly. Ask your direct reports and clients, "To what extent do you use OKR Leadership to drive your business?" Score from 1 (low) to 10 (high) like the Net Promoter Score.
2. What evidence can you provide to demonstrate that you are practicing a growth mindset?
3. How do you know if you are asking great questions? What unsolicited feedback do you receive from your direct reports or clients?
4. Have you shared your OKRs with 10+ stakeholders in your career, team or organization?
5. How are you practicing alignment with your organization's mission, vision and strategy?
6. What is your OKR Leadership accountability cadence?
7. What is your system for practicing AD-FIT™ coaching with your direct reports or clients?

Key points from Chapter 5, OKR Leadership and Career Development

1. OKR Leadership can be a career development process for you to practice what matters next, at any age.
2. A job is defined as the activity that provides you with money and sustenance.
3. A career is defined as a series of jobs that provide you with opportunity, meaning or purpose.
4. A calling is defined as meaningful activities that provide you with meaning or serve a purpose larger than yourself.

5. Career development requires practicing new skills with a new accountability team. Individuals do not win, teams win.

Key questions from Chapter 5, OKR Leadership and Career Development

1. Would you describe your attitude toward work today as a job, career or a calling?
2. How many careers have you had to date? If you were to have three to five more careers, how might you describe those careers? If you were to describe your next career with slashes (e.g., a consultant/writer/teacher or a programmer/CEO), then what could your next three to five careers possibly be?
3. What activity do you do that leads to a flow state (a balance of challenge and skills) that someone would pay you to do?
4. What activity do you do that leads others to state, "Thank you, that was valuable"?
5. How are you serving others today? Specifically, how do you know that you are providing value or quality to others? How many others do you serve each year? How many others do you want to serve next year?
6. How are you providing for your physical needs in the last 20 years of your life? What social support will be ideal? How much money will you need? Where would you like to live?

Key points from Chapter 6, Family Leadership and OKR Leadership

1. The primary objective of this chapter is to define the problem of family leadership for family members, owners and consultants.
2. A secondary objective of this chapter is to provide examples of how you can apply OKR Leadership to a family-owned business
3. Family leaders try their best, but often lack leadership skills.
4. Family-owned business leaders also try their best, and require OKR Leadership to practice what matters next. Examples include succession planning, cost reduction and organizational change.

Key questions from Chapter 6, Family Leadership and OKR Leadership

1. Who are some of the best family leaders you know? What behaviors or values do they demonstrate that makes them so remarkable?
2. Family-owned business leaders often describe confusion about their overlapping roles as family members, managers and owners. Using Figures 11 and 12, how would you advise any family-owned business leaders to become more effective?
3. How can you apply OKR Leadership your family-owned business? Or in your family?

OKR Leadership Fact Sheet

Objectives = What is to be achieved. They are qualitative, subjective, and significant.

Key Results (KRs) = 3-5 quantitative measures that verify the status of any objective with numbers.

OKR Leadership = A process for managers and leaders to practice what matters.

OKR Leadership is:

1. Radical for top-down hierarchical organizations to implement
2. A bridge between silos (e.g., operations and human resources, regional and corporate) that need to share resources or collaborate
3. Individually written by people at any level of a team or organization

OKR Leadership is NOT:

1. Tied to performance reviews, compensation or rewards
2. A new fad or unvalidated approach to decision-making
3. A "silver bullet" for every career, team or organization

Why you could practice OKR Leadership:

1. Align and connect for teamwork
2. Track for accountability and transparency
3. Stretch for amazing innovation
4. Focus resources and commit to priorities
5. Increased agency for individuals and teams

How to develop OKR Leadership:

1. Practice a growth mindset
2. Practice asking great questions
1. 3: Practice sharing your OKRs
3. Practice alignment
4. Practice an accountability cadence
5. Practice AD-FIT™ coaching

Glossary of OKR Leadership terms

AD-FIT™ Model. An evidence-based approach to positive psychology coaching or management consulting based upon (a) awareness of strengths and growth mindset, (b) defining a meaningful objective, (c) focus on the client's agenda, (d) interventions and interactions, (e) takeaways, and (f) percentage of compliance to this model.

Coaching. A collaborative relationship or process designed for coachees to attain meaningful performance or business outcomes (Green & Spence, 2014).

Continuous innovation. The ability to renew an organization and to develop new products and business models.

Culture. How organizations function. Academics describe culture using three overlapping circles and label each circle as: 1) underlying assumptions, 2) espoused behavior, and 3) artifacts. 1) Underlying assumptions are the shared beliefs of an organization including history of acquisitions, traits of key leaders who get promoted faster, competencies of leaders with higher reputations, or those unspoken assumption you have about a market or colleague. 2) Espoused behaviors describe what we say we do, including common phrases such as "I'll solve this" or "that's not my problem." Notice the difference between what we *say* we do, and what we *actually* do.

3) Artifacts are tangible symbols of the culture, such as a new national office for centralized services and consistent management of others. The cultural values posted in the lobby are artifacts of how you work.

Evidence-based coaching. The use of best current knowledge integrated with practitioner expertise when making decisions about how to deliver coaching (Green & Spence, 2014).

Follower Trust Index (FTI). The extent to which you think others in your organization trust you.

Key Result (KR). How to measure and verify any objective with numbers or data. KRs must be specific, time-bound, aggressive yet realistic 60-80% of the time, measurable and verifiable. For example, expectations for clients in my workshops include: KR1: All participants will develop 4-5 objectives (maximum). Each objective will have a different focus (e.g., operational or aspirational, business development, leadership development, career development, regional development, etc.). KR2: Each objective must have 3-5 (maximum) Key Results. These KRs must be specific, time-bound, aggressive yet realistic, measurable and verifiable.

Leadership Trust Index (LTI). The extent to which you trust the leaders in your organization.

Objective. What is to be achieved. Objectives must be significant, concrete, action-oriented behaviors and (ideally) 40% are aspirational. For example, expectations for clients in my workshops include: O1: All participants will develop 4-5 objectives (maximum). Each objective will have a different focus (e.g., operational or aspirational, business development, leadership development, career development, regional development, etc.) O2: Each objective must have 3-5 (maximum) Key Results. These KRs must be specific, time-bound, aggressive yet realistic, measurable and verifiable. O3: Leaders who PRACTICE their objectives will out-perform others by over 100%

OKR Leadership. A process for managers and leaders to practice what matters.

Organizational characteristics. A broad range of factors influencing an organization e.g., values, organization structure, capabilities, leadership, performance and incentive system

Positivity. An integrated system of antecedents, processes, practices and outcomes that can be readily identified and agreed upon by diverse observers and stakeholders as uniquely surpassing standards of adequate functioning and adding sustainable value to both the individual and the context (Yousseff-Morgan & Luthans, 2013).

Positive Organizational Behavior (POB). The study and application of positively oriented human resource strengths and psychological capacities that can be measured, developed and effectively managed for performance improvement in today's workplace (Luthans, 2002).

Positive Organizational Scholarship (POS). The study of positive phenomena at organizational levels. Four aspects of POS research include (1) adopt a unique lens (e.g., problems are not ignored but interpreted as opportunities to generate growth), (2) focus on extraordinary outcomes, (3) focus on growth and positive outcomes, (4) focus on the conditions for optimal flourishing (Cameron & Spreitzer, 2012; Cameron, 2013).

Positive Psychology (PP). The scientific pursuit of optimal human functioning and applied interventions that leverage human strengths (adapted from Seligman, 2002; Gilbert, 2006).

Positive Psychology Coaching (PPC). The practice of coaching combined with a focus on what is right, positive emotions, and signature strengths of a coachee (Biswas-Diener, 2010).

Positive Psychology Consulting. The application of positive psychology to improve a client's condition.

Positive psychology interventions (PPIs). Intentional activities that aim to increase well-being through the cultivation of positive feelings, cognitions and behaviors (Green & Spence, 2014).

Psychological capital (PsyCap). A dynamic, developmental state, and a higher-order construct comprised of four measurable variables: hope, efficacy, resilience, optimism (the HERO-within acronym, Luthans et al., 2015.)

An OKR Leadership quiz

Edit this quiz for your team, organization, or book discussion group.

1. What is the best definition for "objectives" from the list below?

    a. Objectives describe what is critically required for organizational success

    b. Objectives describe what you want to do. They are qualitative and subjective.

    c. Objectives are the hardest imaginable outcomes defined by managers to motivate others.

Best answer: b.

2. What is the best example of a good key result (KR) from the list below?

    a. My KR is to increase my annual bonus at least 25%

    b. My KR is to decrease customer complaints from 100/month to 60/month within 30 days

    c. My KR is to increase productivity year over year

Best answer: b.

3. What is the best use of OKR Leadership?

    a. A pilot case in one division or subset of a large organization

    b. A new startup technology company

    c. Any organization that requires more accountability and transparency

Best answer: c.

4. Why was the title "The Father of OKRs" ascribed to Andy Grove at Intel?

    a. Andy Grove wrote "Only the Paranoid Survive" and a textbook on semiconductors

    b. Andy Grove was an engineer who wanted to systemically organize decision making

    c. All of the above

    d. None of the above

Best answer: c.

5. What is the best example of a KR from the list below?

    a. Work hard every day

    b. Try to meet or exceed my manager's expectations

    c. Make at least 3 sales calls to identified targets every hour and record the results in salesforce

Best answer: c.

6. What is the best definition for "objectives" from the list below?

    a. Increase EBITDA and share price

    b. Retain 90% of desired employees in this calendar year

    c. Reduce waste from $100k/year to $80k/year by the end of the fiscal year

Best answer: b.

7. What is the best application for OKR Leadership in your organization?

    a. Anywhere the senior leadership team wants to implement them

    b. In a low-performing division that is struggling to achieve performance outcomes

c. Anywhere we need to increase accountability and transparency
d. Only with millennials working on innovative projects

Best answer: c.

8. Why does OKR Leadership work in organizations?

   a. John Doerr made an $11.8M investment in 12% of Google when working as a venture capitalist at Kleiner-Perkins.
   b. The co-founders of Google needed to adopt a management decision-making process to organize data globally.
   c. Applied business psychologists like Martin Seligman know that people flourish when they focus on their strengths.
   d. OKR Leadership does not work in all organizations. It requires executive sponsorship and leaders willing to practice leadership.

Best answer: d.

9. How is OKR Leadership the secret sauce for Silicon Valley?

a) It accelerates innovation at technology companies like Google, Intuit, Adobe and any organization

b) It accelerates trillions of dollars in venture capital funding since the 1970s

c) It provides agency (a sense of control) for brilliant workers with abundant career choices

d) All of the above

Best answer: d

10. How is OKR Leadership the secret sauce for management consulting?

a) It increases engagement and agency (a sense of control)
b) It increases risk-taking and innovation
c) It requires that people measure activities, which models accountability and transparency
d) All of the above

Best answer: d

11. Do OKRs only work well in technology-based organizations such as Google?

a) Yes. The roots are in agile software, therefore OKR Leadership can only work in technology-based organizations.
b) No. OKR Leadership can work in any type of organization.

Best answer: b

12. Teams that implement OKR Leadership out-perform individuals that implement OKR Leadership. True or False?

a) Yes, true. OKR Leadership is a team activity.
b) No, false. Individuals are rewarded for their performance and behavior.

Best answer: a

13. OKR Leadership is defined as a process for managers to practice leading what matters. Which of these is the best example of OKR Leadership?

   a) We will track gross revenue quarterly and reward new sales with a 1% commission incentive in Q2
   b) We will reward each business unit with a 6% profit margin and a 2% reduction in expenses in Q4
   c) We will build a lunar module weighing under 40,000 pounds by December 1965
   d) All of the above
   e) None of the above

Best answer: d

14. What is the best definition for leadership?

   a) Knowing your why.
   b) Working hard to get results.
   c) Influencing others' behavior.

Best answer: c

15. Key Results (KRs) are defined as the 3-5 measures of each objective. They are quantitative and measurable. Which of the following are examples of good KRs?

   a) We will drive for 7 hours a day until we arrive in Chicago,
   b) We will track gross revenue quarterly and reward new sales with a 1% commission incentive in Q2,
   c) We will reward each business unit with a 6% profit margin and a 2% reduction in expenses in Q4.
   d) All of the above

Best answer: d

16. There are two types of objectives, operational objectives and aspirational objectives. What is the best answer from the options below?

a) Operational objectives are the important activities to maintain your business.
b) Aspirational objectives are the important activities to transform your business.
c) Leaders should strive for 60% aspirational objectives on your team to encourage innovation.
d) All of the above

Best answer: d

DIGITAL RESOURCES
ON OKR LEADERSHIP

Share these links with your team, organization,
or book discussion group.

1. For all individual and organization leadership consulting and executive coaching services see www.Action-Learning.com

2. I created a series of short videos on OKR Leadership that can be found at www.Action-Learning.com > Free Courses tab on the header. They are hosted at https://www.youtube.com/channel/UCvBbVpkJbgKKdZuP 05bX00Q?view_as=subscriber

3. For a keynote address excerpt, see the 3-minute video introduction to OKR Leadership from an address to over 700 leaders at https://action-learning.com/about/ or at https://www.youtube.com/watch?v=9_duHp51RIA&t=2s

4. For 1.5 Continuing Education (CE) credits I developed a digital OKR Leadership course at https://www.illumeo.com/courses/objectives-key-results-okr-leadership-training

5. For global executive and leadership coaching go to www.CoachSource.com and mention Doug Gray or this book

6. For the Family Business Consulting Group go to www.TheFBCG.com and mention Doug Gray or this book

7. For AD-FIT™ coaching certification go to www.ADFIT.org

8. For videos, workshops and bulk book orders go to www.OKRLeadership.com

REFERENCES

Aronoff, C.E., Mc Clure, S.L., & Ward, J.L. (2011). *Family Business Succession; The final test of greatness.* Palgrave Macmillan; New York.

Bork, D., Jaffe, D.T., Lane, S.H., Dashew, L., & Heisler, Q.G. (1996). *Working with family businesses; A guide for professionals.* Jossey-Bass; San Francisco.

Brun de Pontet, S., Aronoff, C.E., Mendoza, D.S., & Ward, J.L. (2012). *Siblings and the family business; Making it work for business, the family, and the future.* Palgrave Macmillan; New York.

Burke, W.W. (2014). *Organizational Change; Theory and Practice, 4th ed.* Sage Publications; Los Angeles.

Doerr, J. (2018). *Measure what Matters; How Google, Bono and the Gates Foundation rock the world with OKRs.* Penguin; New York.

Girard, B. (2009). *The Google Way; How one company is revolutionizing management as we know it.* No Starch Press; San Francisco, CA.

Gray, D.W. (2018). Dissertation: *Positive Psychology Coaching Protocols; Creating Competitive Advantage for Leader Development.* ProQuest; Ann Arbor, MI.

Kotter, J.P. (1996). *Leading change.* Harvard Business School Press; Boston.

Mello, F.S.H. (2019) *OKRs, from mission to metrics; How objectives and key results can help your company achieve great things.* Publisher unknown.

Niven, P.R. & Lamorte, B. (2016). *Objectives and key results; Driving focus, alignment and engagement with OKRs.* Wiley; Hoboken, NJ.

Pearson, T. (2019). *Goal setting and team management with OKR objectives and key results; Smart project management skills for effective office leadership, business focus and growth.* Publisher unknown.

Pink, D. (2011). *Drive: The Surprising Truth About What Motivates Us.* Riverhead; New York.

Poole, M.S. & Hollingshed, A.B., Eds. (2005). *Theories of Small Groups, Interdisciplinary Perspectives.* Sage Publications, Thousand Oaks, CA.

Seligman, M.E.P. (2011). *Flourish; A visionary new understanding of happiness and well-being.* Simon & Schuster; New York.

Steiber, A. & Alange, S. (2013). "A corporate system for continuous innovation: the case of Google Inc." *European Journal of Innovation and Management, 16*(2), 243-264.

Wodtke, C. (2016). Radical Focus; Achieving your most important goals with objectives and key results. Publisher unknown.

ACKNOWLEDGEMENTS

Good leaders, like artists, copy from others; but great leaders steal from others and PRACTICE what works. This book is a result of countless people practicing leadership. Some are listed below. Some are my family and friends and clients Just like you, *all* leaders influence others' behavior toward a better future. These leaders have certainly helped me develop my practice. I am grateful beyond words. Thank you each for sharing your hopes and objectives with me.

The primary contributors for this book include my clients and colleagues.

Action Learning Associates, LLC, was founded in 1997 and has served over 10,000 individual and organizational clients in multiple business sectors. Confidentiality for those clients was protected in this text by using fictional names to protect their anonymity. You know *who* you are and *what* you have accomplished. Thank you for trusting the OKR Leadership process. Your successes are a result of your resilience and practice.

Colleagues who edited and provided testimonials for this text include John Mattox, PhD, Justin Jude, Brian Underhill, PhD, Terry Fortner, Craig Aronoff, PhD, Sheri Bankston, Dave Vance, PhD, James Dillon, Bill Ryan, PhD, David Cardwell, and Jac Fitzenz, PhD. Thank you each for your generosity and service to practicing leadership.

Colleagues who contributed to this text include Patrick McLean, Joe Baker, Chuck Scharenberg, Tom Lemanski, Deanne Priddis, PhD, Willy Steiner, Josh Bersin, Lonnie Morris, PhD, and Fred Jones, EdD. Thank you each for sharing your expertise.

Teams create products, not individuals. I appreciate the editorial services of Christine Moore, Dan Alexander and the team at NY Book Editors. I also appreciate the book cover and formatting expertise of Dane Low and the team at eBookLaunch. And I appreciate the graphic design skills of John Murdock. Thank you each for making this content accessible to readers on any device.

ABOUT THE AUTHOR

Doug Gray, PhD, PCC has always focused on outcome-based leader development. He has worked with over 10,000 leaders in multiple business sectors, schools and colleges, families and non-profits. Since 1997, as CEO of Action Learning Associates, www.action-learning.com, his consultancy guarantees results using the globally validated AD-FIT™ protocol in workshops, assessments and executive coaching. Doug speaks and trains leaders throughout North America. This is his third book, written because his clients asked, "What *really* works?"

Doug and his family live near Nashville, TN, USA.

CONSULTING SERVICES

Workshops, assessments, executive coaching and speaking services.

See www.Action-Learning.com for all individual and organizational leadership consulting, family business consulting, training workshops, assessments, and executive coaching services

See www.ADFIT.org for free and paid digital training programs

See www.OKRLeadership.com for OKR workshops, speaking and bulk book orders

Contact Doug Gray at www.Action-Learning.com or 615.236.9845 today

Thank you for practicing OKR Leadership.

Made in USA - Kendallville, IN
1051562_9780975884164
02.28.2020 0804